Eco Chic
organic living

THIS IS A CARLTON BOOK

Design and special photography copyright ©
2000 Carlton Books Limited
Text copyright © 2000 Rebecca Tanqueray
This edition was published by Carlton Books
Limited in 2000
20 Mortimer Street
London W1N 7RD

This book is sold subject to the condition that it
shall not, by way of trade or otherwise, be lent,
resold, hired out or otherwise circulated
without the publisher's prior written consent in
any form of cover or binding other than that in
which it is published and without a similar
condition including this condition being
imposed upon the subsequent purchaser.

All rights reserved
A CIP catalogue for this book is available from
the British Library
ISBN 1 85868 984 8

Editorial Manager: Venetia Penfold
Art Director: Penny Stock
Designer: Liz Lewis at LewisHallam
Project Editor: Zia Mattocks
Copy Editors: Jo Lethaby and Alice Whately
Picture Researcher: Abi Dillon
Special photography: Janine Hosegood
Production Controller: Janette Davis

Printed and bound in Spain

Eco Chic
organic living

REBECCA TANQUERAY

CARLTON
BOOKS

	eating	lounging	working
	8	36	66
INTRODUCTION	**THE KITCHEN**	**THE LIVING SPACE**	**THE OFFICE**
6	10	38	68
	THE FOOD	**URBAN ECO**	**ECO TECHNO**
	20	50	72
	THE DRINK		**ECO OFFICE KIT**
	30		76

bathing · sleeping & dressing · outdoors

82 · 108 · 126

THE BATHROOM
84

THE BEDROOM
110

THE HOUSE
128

RESOURCES
142

ECO BEAUTY
96

ECO DRESSING
118

THE GARDEN
138

INDEX
143

COMPLEMENTARY MEDICINE
100

ACKNOWLEDGEMENTS
144

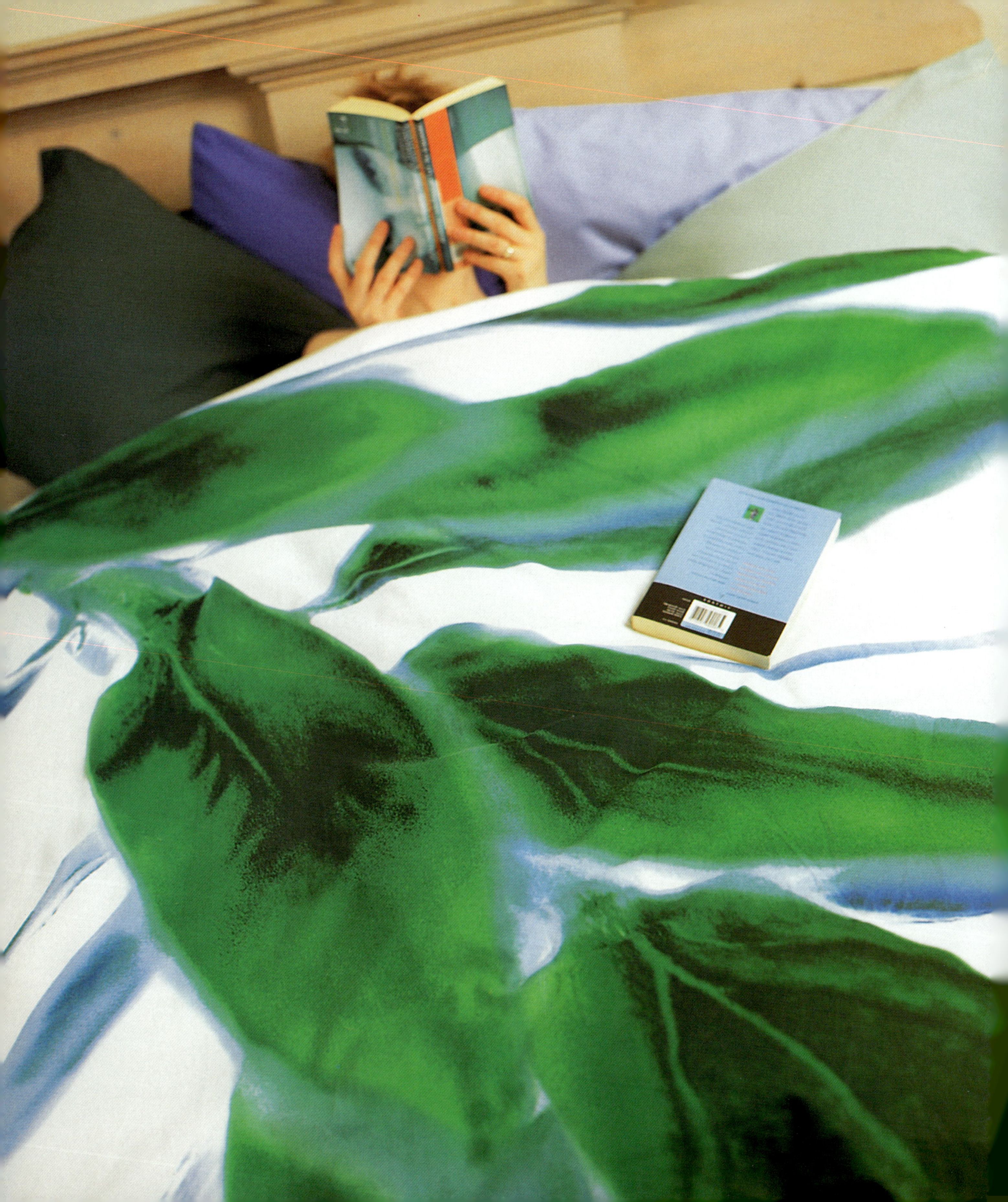

introduction

Living an eco-friendly lifestyle has at last become hip. While twenty or even ten years ago environmental awareness was something that was left to the experts or eccentrics, today, as we start the new millennium, it has become a key issue for all of us. As the harmful side-effects of consumerism and mass production become more apparent and start to impinge on our own lives, many of us are becoming much more open to the bonuses of living in tune with nature rather than against it.

Part of the reason for the change is that the green movement, spreading right across the Western hemisphere, has developed from a marginal political force into something far more accessible. Kick-started by global concerns about health and pollution, eco living is now something we can embrace in the privacy of our own homes – an alternative lifestyle option that can be just as much about personal choice (what to eat; what to wear; where to sleep) as political goals.

But the main reason why eco is suddenly chic is that it has lost its earthy and earnest image. It is no longer simply about brown rice and compost toilets (although they still have a part to play); it has come to be a fashion statement. As big name celebrities and style-conscious young urbanites convert to the green cause – embracing organic eating, natural health and eco fashion, for example – so it has become the trendy option for the rest of us, with an 'eco look' for the home being the latest word in style.

Just how far you choose to take either the look or the lifestyle is, of course, entirely up to you. You may simply switch to an organic diet or dabble in alternative medicine; you may go all out to convert your home with eco-friendly furniture, furnishings and fittings. Just remember that the more you do, the bigger will be your contribution to the health and the future of the planet.

eating

Nothing is more important than food. It's a gift from the earth, a pleasure to be shared, the stuff of life. And yet, over the past hundred years or so, in the Western world particularly, we have divorced food from nature and turned it into a man-made commodity. We have manufactured it, processed it, packaged and modified it, turning what should be a natural product into a giant and polluting industry. Animals are farmed intensively to create large quantities of low-cost meat; fruit and vegetables are sprayed with chemicals to increase output; even at home, our super-efficient kitchens are wasting water and energy – natural resources that are becoming increasingly precious. Adopting an eco-friendly attitude to food is no longer simply a lifestyle choice but a necessity. The good news is, it will benefit not only the environment but ourselves, too.

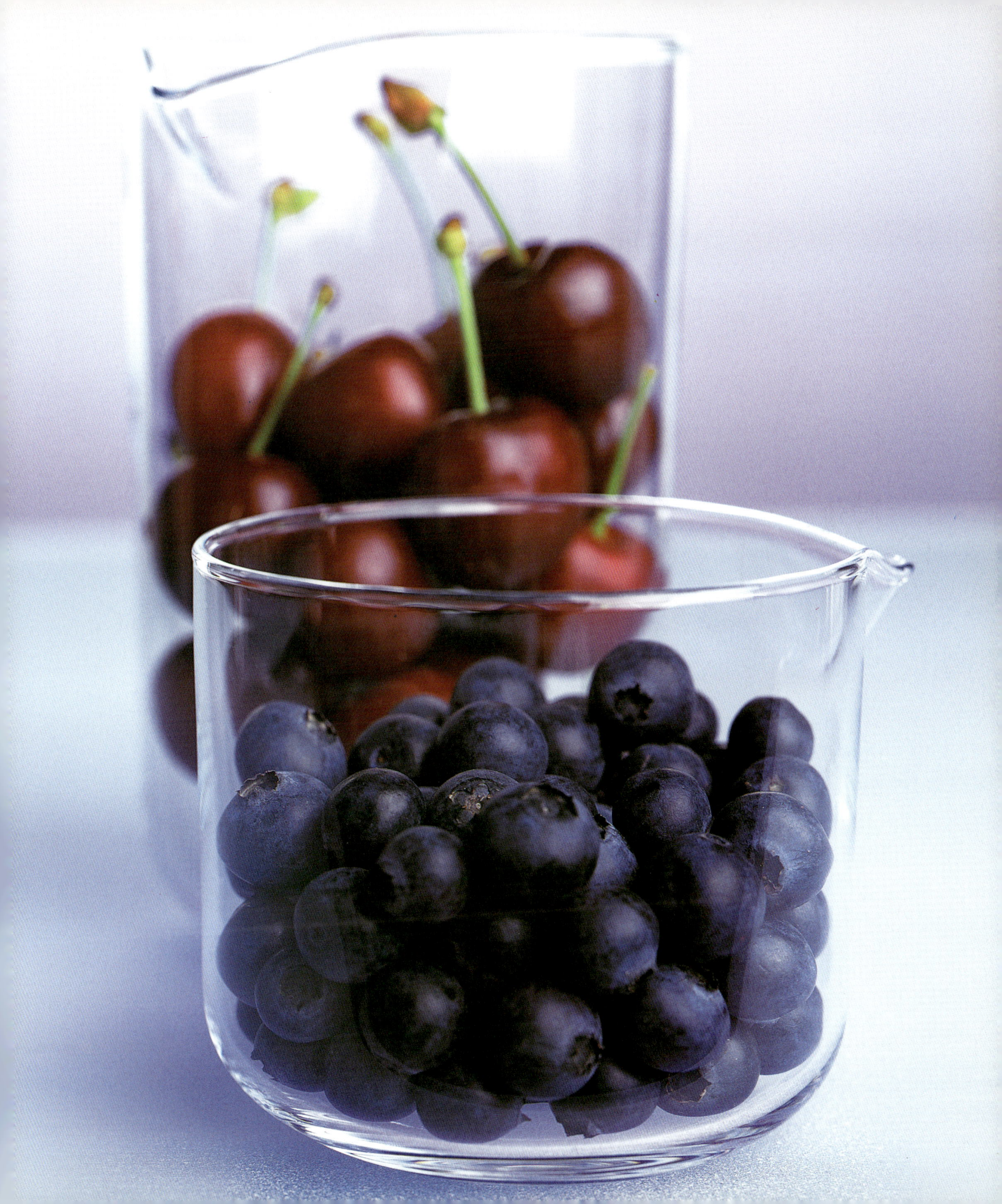

the kitchen

Adopting eco-friendly principles in the kitchen is not as hard in practice as it may sound. Being green does not mean chucking out your up-to-the-minute gadgets and doing everything by hand – indeed the reverse is often more true. It is simply a matter of becoming aware of your impact on the world around you.

You may think that if you change to an organic diet, you are doing your bit for the green cause, but there are countless other ways to be eco-friendly in the kitchen. Look around you. Is your washing machine pumping out litres of water? Is your cooker wasting energy? Is your bin full of non-biodegradable plastic bags? As a consumer, every aspect of your life has an effect on the planet; the kitchen is a prime spot for eco nasties, so spend a little time considering how you can alter your environment for the benefit of the wider one.

Adopting eco-friendly principles in the kitchen is not as hard in practice as it may sound. Being green does not mean chucking out your up-to-the-minute gadgets and doing everything by hand – indeed the reverse is often more true. Designing and using your kitchen with the environment in mind can be achieved with minimum disruption to your lifestyle and maximum benefit to your health as well as that of the planet. It is simply a matter of becoming aware of your impact on the world around you and approaching kitchen tasks with a little more conscience than before.

Think about using environmentally friendly materials in the design of the space; choose low-energy appliances and abandon harmful chemical products in favour of natural ones. Consider recycling packaging and bottles before you throw them into the bin. Small individual contributions to the health of the planet can, cumulatively, have a global impact.

design

The idea of environmentally-friendly design might initially conjure up images of the pseudo-country look of the early 1990s – rough wooden furniture, bunches of dried flowers and twiggy accessories. There was a green element involved, of course, but today's eco kitchen does not have to conform to that dated and rustic natural look; it can be as chic and urban as any of its contemporary counterparts. And if you are about to change the floor, install new units or update your appliances, it makes sense to choose designs and materials that are stylish and green.

FLOORS AND SURFACES

The key here is to choose materials that will do least harm both to the planet and to you. Be discerning. Ask manufacturers and suppliers where they source their products and, if man-made, exactly what they

THE CONTEMPORARY KITCHEN CAN EMBRACE MODERN DESIGN WITHOUT COMPROMISING ITS ECO CREDENTIALS. A NATURAL WOODEN WORKTOP (OPPOSITE) GIVES CUTTING-EDGE LOOKS WITHOUT HARMING THE ENVIRONMENT, WHILE SLEEK WOODEN BOWLS (BELOW) ARE PERFECT FOR HEALTHY ECO EATING AND ARE ALSO THE HEIGHT OF FASHION.

contain. With a little research, you should be able to get the look you want without compromising your style or the environment. (See page 44 for further flooring ideas.)

WOOD

As a renewable, natural and versatile material, wood is the obvious choice for a kitchen floor or worktop, but make sure you choose timber that comes from a sustainable source (see page 131). If you are buying new, avoid endangered tropical hardwoods such as teak, or try and source reclaimed timber from a local salvage yard. A better alternative is to choose a temperate hardwood, like American oak or European beech which are grown in managed forests, or the quicker growing softwoods, such as pine or spruce, although these two may not be suitable for surfaces that will get lots of wear and tear. If you really want a dark, tropical-looking wood, simply use wood stain.

CERAMIC, STONE AND STEEL

Solid, durable and non-polluting, ceramic tiles and stone work well as worktop surfaces or on the floor. Choose local materials if you can to avoid the energy wasted in transportation or, better still, opt for salvaged samples to avoid depleting natural resources, which may be abundant today, but which are non-renewable.

Choose a variety which will suit the look you want – a sleek slab of limestone or granite for a clean-lined, cutting-edge kitchen; colourful glazed tiles or even mosaic for something more decorative. If you do opt for granite, however, be aware that it sometimes contains high levels of Radon – a radioactive gas – and might need to be tested before use.

Steel uses energy in its engineering and can be extremely expensive, but it scores fairly highly as far as the environment is concerned. It, too, is non-polluting and much of it is made with iron recycled from scrap. If you are after a minimal, modern kitchen, this is the choice for you.

DESIGNED WITH A WEALTH OF NATURAL, RECYCLED AND REAPPROPRIATED MATERIALS, THIS HOUSE IN CHILE IS AS ECO-FRIENDLY AS YOU CAN GET. A COMBINATION OF WOOD, STONE AND SEASIDE SALVAGE, THE INTERIOR LOOKS IN TUNE WITH THE NATURAL WORLD WITHOUT BEING TWEE.

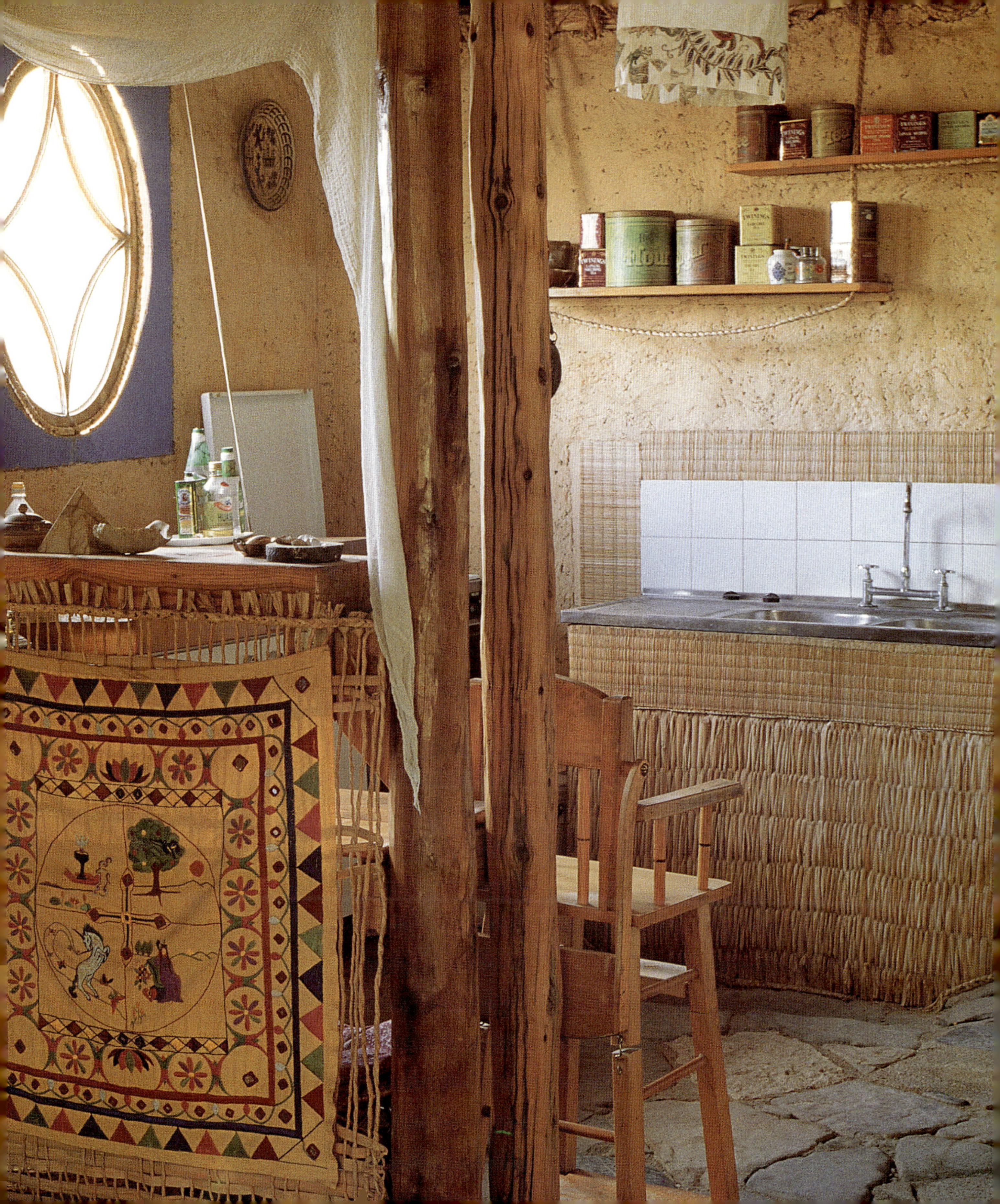

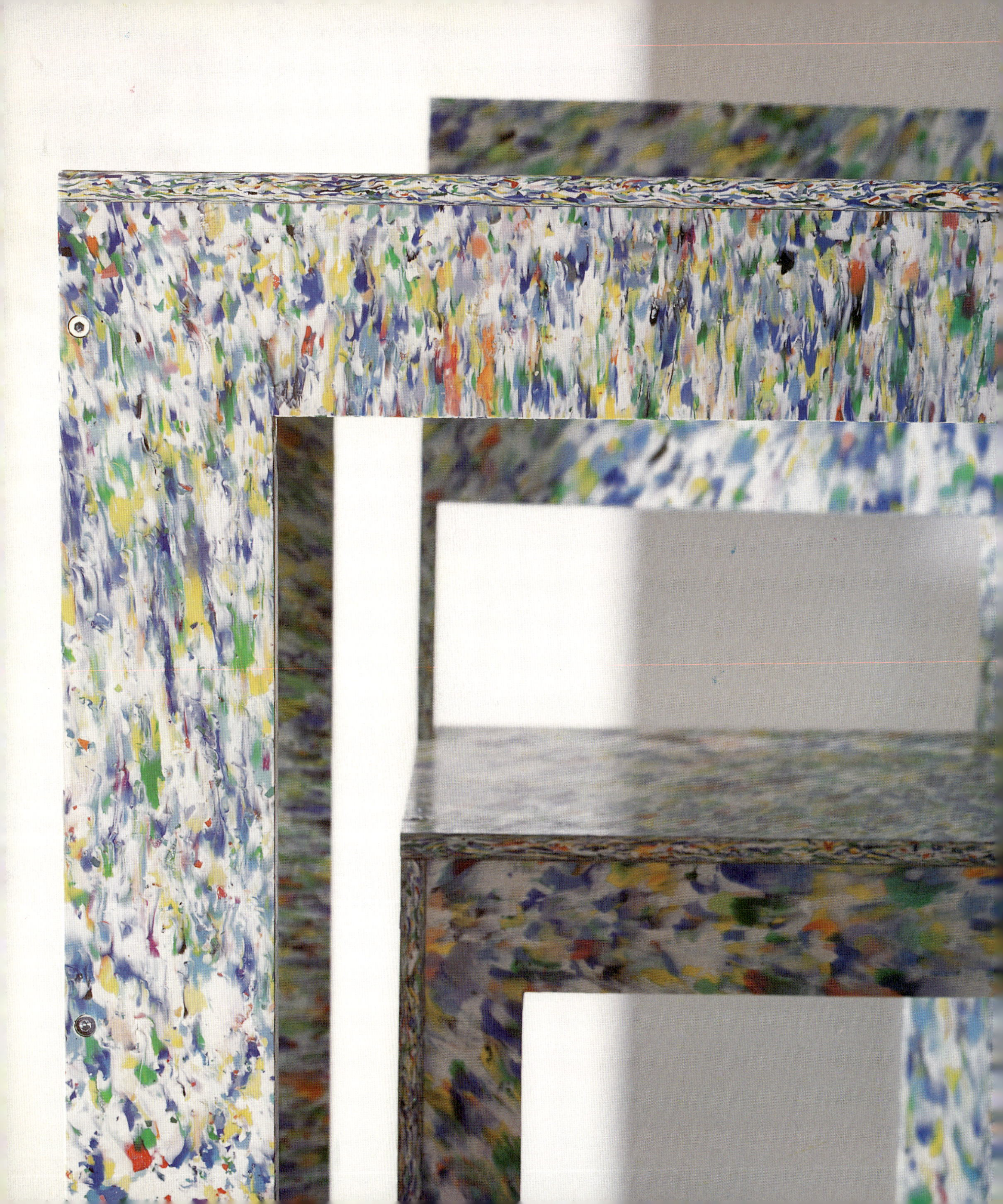

PLASTICS, PLYWOODS AND PARTICLEBOARDS

These materials have taken over in the home in recent years. Easy to manipulate and cheap to make, they seemed the ideal materials for low-cost, contemporary and creative kitchen design. As far as the planet – and your health – is concerned, however, they are not such good news. Some particleboards and plywoods may contain formaldehyde, a suspected carcinogen, which can escape and contaminate the surrounding air if the material is not effectively sealed with paint or varnish (organic, of course).

Some plastics, particularly vinyl and soft plastics, can also contain harmful chemicals and 'offgas' (continue to give off vapours), particularly in warm and humid environments. In addition, few plastics are completely biodegradable, although progress is being made in this respect and some smaller products, such as bin and carrier bags, are now being made from biodegradable materials.

If you must use plastic in the design of your kitchen, seek out the most eco-friendly one you can find; alternatively, consider using sheets of recycled plastic. Made from empty bottles of shampoo, detergent and so on, this plastic looks like synthetic marble, comes in a variety of colours – depending on the bottles used in the mix – and will give a trendy touch to any functional space. Although not particularly eco-friendly in itself, by reusing plastics that would otherwise be discarded, this recycled sheeting does make some contribution towards the reduction of harmful chemical waste.

If your kitchen is already kitted out with all or any of these materials, do not feel you have to strip them all out immediately or start cooking in a gas mask. If they are effectively sealed and the area is well ventilated, it is unlikely that you will suffer any ill effects unless you are very chemically sensitive.

BRITISH DESIGNER JANE ATFIELD BROUGHT RECYCLED PLASTIC TO THE FOREFRONT OF HOME FURNISHINGS WITH A BRILLIANT COLLECTION OF CONTEMPORARY FURNITURE (LEFT) – ENTITLED 'MADE OF WASTE'. MADE OF EMPTY HOUSEHOLD BOTTLES, THE RECYCLED PLASTIC SHEETS SHE USED FOR HER FURNITURE COME IN VARIOUS COLOURS AND WIDTHS AND CAN BE USED ELSEWHERE IN THE HOME, TOO – AS A FUNKY WORKTOP, A PSYCHEDELIC SCREEN OR EVEN ON THE FLOOR.

ACCESSORIES AND COOKWARE

The trick here is to stick to the simple items: china and glass bowls, wooden spoons, steel saucepans – things that most of us have already. Plastics, of course, are tempting. They are cheap, cheerful and brilliant for adding a splash of colour, but they simply cannot match the eco credentials of good old-fashioned cooking utensils.

The idea of banishing plastics completely is unrealistic in today's kitchen, where they proliferate. Consider easy-seal containers, electric kettles, washing-up bowls, sieves, clingfilm – the list is endless. Instead, try and limit their use by substituting plastic products for eco alternatives where you can. David Pearson in his *The New Natural House Book* gives these tips:

- Avoid products with plastic packaging, bags and non-returnable bottles. Reuse shopping bags and baskets.
- Opt for alternative materials and non-plastic products when possible.
- Don't use plastics, particularly soft ones, for storing food or drink, nor plastic water pipes for drinking supplies. (My note: the plasticizers in PVC clingfilm can leach into fatty and warm foods, so use greaseproof paper or cellophane for wrapping these instead.)
- Campaign for proper recycling.

THINKING GREEN

You won't be able to change your kitchen overnight, but you can change your attitude in an instant, which is, at least, half the battle. Make a conscious choice always to try and buy green products and you will find that there are many chic eco-kitchen products available to choose from: recycled glasses (glass can be recycled over and over again with no visible reduction in its quality), coconut-shell bowls, bamboo mats and, best of all, totally biodegradable plates made from leaves – the perfect tableware for a truly organic supper.

ALUMINIUM

Another kitchen nasty is aluminium. Not only does its production require huge amounts of energy and take a raw material (bauxite) from rainforest areas, it can also leach from saucepans and foil into acidic foods and may cause health problems. These days there are few bare aluminium pans around (if you have some, replace them with stainless steel alternatives), but for most people foil has become a necessity in the kitchen – something they cannot imagine doing without. The only solution is to use it more sparingly and substitute greaseproof paper in its place when you can.

GET THE ORGANIC LOOK IN
THE KITCHEN BY INTRODUCING
ROUNDED SHAPES AND NATURAL
TEXTURES, AND KEEP YOUR
CUPBOARDS FREE FROM ECO
NASTIES. INSTEAD OF CHEAP
PLASTIC ACCESSORIES (WHICH
MAY POLLUTE YOU AND THE
ENVIRONMENT), CHOOSE
TABLEWARE WHICH IS GOOD-
LOOKING AND GREEN: PLAIN
CHINA BOWLS, TERRACOTTA
PLATES OR SIMPLE WOODEN
CUTLERY ARE IDEAL. PARED
DOWN AND MODERN, THESE
BEAUTIFUL BASICS WILL
BRING A NATURAL INTEGRITY
AND A SENSE OF SOUL TO ANY
CONTEMPORARY KITCHEN.

GREEN MACHINES

The modern gadget-filled kitchen is the prime spot for energy and water wastage in the home but what can we do about it? Even the most eco-conscious among us would find it difficult to countenance life without some of our labour-saving devices – a fridge, say, or a washing machine. The answer is we don't have to. These days, manufacturers worldwide are starting to produce efficient, stylish kitchen machines with good environmental ratings – suppliers and stores should be able to give you the relevant information. By buying and using appliances responsibly, we can do a great deal to lessen the impact of our consumption on the environment.

COOKERS

Opt for a gas cooker if possible because it uses less energy and causes less environmental pollution than an electric one (gas production releases far less carbon dioxide into the atmosphere than electricity production). To avoid indoor pollution, install a cooker hood with an extractor fan or open the windows. Remember, too, that a full oven is more energy efficient than an empty one; and that a steamer can halve or even third energy consumption on the hob.

WASHING MACHINES

These use huge amounts of water and energy, so if you are about to invest in a new one, make sure it has a good energy rating – look for the EU Ecolabel in Europe, the Green Seal in the USA or the equivalent elsewhere. Also, you should try to buy one with a low wattage and avoid machines that use cold water only as heating takes more energy.

If you are not buying new, reduce the wastage of your existing machine by avoiding half loads and by investing in a few eco gadgets – a washing disc that treats the water and allows you to wash at lower temperatures, for example, or a magnetic ball to improve the performance of your machine by preventing a build-up of calcium.

The other problem with washing machines is what we put in them – other than clothes, that is. Your favourite powder no doubt 'washes whiter' because, like most conventional powders and detergents, it contains bleach to remove stains and phosphates to soften the water. The latter are particularly harmful because they are non-biodegradable and continue to pollute waterways long after their use. However, effective phosphate-free powders are available and, although they may cost more, you need less of them so they should last longer.

DISHWASHERS

These days the most efficient machines use less water than it takes to wash up by hand for a family of four, so away with the rubber gloves! Older models, however, are not so good and any dishwasher will use

STEPS TO REDUCE YOUR HOUSEHOLD RUBBISH

- Give old clothes, toys and accessories to charity rather than throwing them in the bin.
- Buy less prepackaged food. Packaging materials account for almost a third of household rubbish.
- Buy products in glass rather than plastic bottles and, when empty, return to the shop or take to a bottle bank.
- Put suitable kitchen waste (vegetable peelings, tea, ground coffee and crushed eggshells) on a compost heap if you have one.
- Reuse plastic bags for shopping or, better still, take your own shopping basket with you.
- Sort your rubbish into categories and recycle what you can – paper, cardboard and cans as well as bottles.

LEFT: GREEN MACHINES CAN BE AS CHIC AS THE REST, BUT IF YOU HAVE PROBLEMS FINDING AN APPLIANCE THAT IS ECO-FRIENDLY AND STYLISH, HIDE IT BEHIND A STAINLESS STEEL FACADE.

RIGHT: ECO-FRIENDLY WASHING POWDER IS AVAILABLE FROM MOST SUPERMARKETS.

a lot of energy. The eco tips here are simple common sense: don't run the machine unless it is full, choose an economy programme and be sure to use phosphate-free biodegradable detergent.

FRIDGES AND FREEZERS

If you are buying new, choose one that is free of harmful CFCs – chlorofluorocarbons that deplete the ozone layer and speed up the greenhouse effect – and also one that is low-energy rated. Place both fridge and freezer in as cool a place as you can to conserve energy; keep them well stocked and defrost regularly.

ECO CLEANING

We have all been wooed by advertisers to believe that dirt is bad; that we have to scrub and polish our homes until they sparkle and smell overpoweringly of woodland pine. There are two issues here. Firstly, a bit of dirt never hurt anyone (ask your granny) and secondly, most conventional cleaners on the market are full of chemicals. Far from making your house healthier, these are liable to do the opposite – as well as doing extensive damage to the environment with both their contents and their packaging. As David Pearson says in *The New Natural House Book*: 'Hygiene is obviously important, but there is no point using products that leave surfaces with a "sparkling clean" shine disguising a residual slick of harmful chemicals.'

So next time you rush for a box of disinfectant wipes or a bottle of bleach, consider alternative ways of cleaning instead. Eco-friendly household cleaners – those that do not contain petrochemicals, phosphates, optical brighteners, synthetic perfumes or colourings – are widely available these days and most supermarkets stock one or two brands. Alternatively, if you don't want to pay that little bit extra, go back to basics instead. Common store cupboard products such as vinegar and bicarbonate of soda (sodium bicarbonate) can clean your house very efficiently from top to bottom without hurting anyone.

RUBBISH

Waste is becoming a pressing global problem. Landfill sites are running out and incineration can do more harm than good. The only solution is to reduce the amount of rubbish we produce in the first place, (see above left).

EATING 19

the food

Suddenly, that once-eccentric alternative, organic food, seems highly desirable and the fashion for eating green is gaining momentum by the day. Choosing to buy and eat organically is no longer seen as a hippie fad but as the moral, sensible and stylish food option for consumers everywhere.

These days we consumers are a demanding lot. We want strawberries in winter, ready-washed salads, cheap chickens that we can throw in the oven and microwave meals we can cook in minutes. It seems we no longer have time for real food; we simply want edible products that will fit in with our stressful lifestyles and busy schedules.

Thanks to technology and many willing manufacturers, we have been given just what we want: food that is uniform, abundant and convenient. But suddenly, we have realized that all is not as good as it seems on the supermarket shelves. Those perfectly round, red apples have been treated with chemicals to help them ripen; that shiny 'fresh' fish has been in transit for days; those low-cost chickens have been pumped with antibiotics to make them plump.

Recent food-oriented health scares (BSE and E coli, for example) have focused our minds on the hidden dangers of mass production and overprocessing. They have made many of us, shocked to discover the extent to which our food was being tampered with, reassess our relationship with the things we eat. We want convenient food, yes, but we also want food that is unadulterated and nutritious.

It is not only a health issue. The conventional food industry is doing enormous damage to the environment. Intensive farming is wiping out vast areas of the countryside, tons of (often non-biodegradable) food packaging is contributing to the problem of global waste, and pesticides are polluting our waterways.

Suddenly, that once-eccentric alternative, organic food, seems highly desirable and the fashion for eating green is gaining momentum by the day. As the only way to guarantee a healthy diet and a healthy planet, choosing to buy and eat organically is no longer seen as a hippie fad but as the moral, sensible and stylish food option for consumers everywhere.

WHAT TO EAT
Piles of beansprouts and brown rice, hearty bowls of lentil soup, dense brown bread – these used to be the images that came to mind when we thought about healthy eating. While raw and unrefined foods are indeed far better for us – and the planet – than their more processed relations, you don't have to eat wholefoods alone these days to have a healthy, eco-friendly diet.

Buying organic food – food that is grown and reared without the presence of harmful chemicals – is another way of ensuring that you do as little damage as possible to both yourself and the environment. The wide choice of organic products available today should satisfy even the most sophisticated consumer. While ten, or even as little as five, years ago the organic section in most supermarkets consisted of a few muddy carrots and potatoes and a handful of misshapen apples and unripe pears, today's organic ranges encompass everything from exotic fruits and rich ice creams to smoked salmon and good-quality champagne. What's more, the choice is increasing all the time.

WHAT IS ORGANIC FOOD?
- Organic food is produced using no artificial chemicals, fertilizers or pesticides. Animals are reared free-range and not routinely pumped full of hormones to make them bigger or antibiotics to make them disease-free. (Indeed, even when they are ill, they are often treated with homeopathy and natural remedies.)
- Vegetables and fruits are grown by traditional and natural farming methods – using crop rotation, for example, or biological pesticides – and all organic food is free of genetically modified ingredients.
- To make completely sure that the food you buy is organic, look out for the labelling on it. 'Organic' is a legal definition and all products must be certified by a government-approved body and carry its logo.
- There are several organic accreditation bodies in many countries around the world today (the Soil Association in the UK, for example), all of which must conform to standards set down by the International Federation of Organic Agricultural Movements (IFOAM). Indeed, many of them set even more stringent standards.

organic

nutritious

healthy

fresh

WHERE TO SHOP

At one time, health-food shops used to be tiny 'alternative' places, selling wholesome, earthy food to wholesome, earthy people, but as demand has increased for organic and natural foods, so retail outlets have expanded. Whole Foods Market in America, for example, was founded in 1980 with one small store in Austin, Texas; today the company has more than 100 stores right across the USA and sales of around US$1.6 billion; their competitor, Wild Oats, is just as big and growing equally fast.

With their familiar supermarket formats, these one-stop organic superstores have succeeded in bringing organic and natural foods into the mass market, and conventional supermarkets have been quick to jump on the bandwagon. Most now offer a good range of organic produce and some take the job of eco food very seriously indeed. British supermarket chain J Sainsbury, for example, has plans to turn one of the Windward Islands in the Caribbean into a giant organic farm, capable of producing enough fruit for every one of its UK stores. This strategy will also remove the common problem of cross-pollination from non-organic crops.

ALTERNATIVE SHOPPING

While organic produce is now far more widely available than it used to be, if you do not have a local organic retailer and it is proving difficult to track one down in your area, there are alternative ways of getting hold of it. Organic meats can be bought by mail order, for instance, and boxes of vegetables and fruits can be delivered to your door by one of a growing number of organic suppliers. You can even order produce on the Internet. When it is this simple to get hold of natural and organic food, why make do with the conventional, chemically grown alternatives?

SEEK INSPIRATION FOR YOUR ORGANIC SHOPPING LIST FROM FASHIONABLE ECO EATERIES SUCH AS LOVE IN LONDON (BELOW RIGHT), AND GET CREATIVE IN THE KITCHEN. COOKING WITH WHOLESOME AND UNADULTERATED ORGANIC INGREDIENTS SHOULD MEAN THAT EVEN THE SIMPLEST FOODS WILL TASTE SUBLIME.

THE COST QUESTION

You may have to pay a little more for organic food than its conventional counterparts as it is more labour intensive to produce food without the use of chemicals, and the produce is more highly perishable. That said, if you consider that you are buying a quality alternative, the price differential will not seem so steep. As Renée Elliott, founder of London organic superstore, Planet Organic, comments: 'If you compare organic ice cream, say, with a cheap supermarket own-brand, the organic product will be expensive; but if you compare it with a quality product, like Häagen-Dazs, the likelihood is that it will be cheaper.'

YEAR-ROUND CHOICE

The other issue that can be a stumbling block for would-be converts to organic food is availability. 'We've got used to a food distribution culture which offers us a bewildering choice all year round and it's hard to break the habit,' says food writer Brian Glover. 'But year-round availability is an artificial construct and it is part of the point of organic food that peaks and troughs appear.' The seasonality of fruits and vegetables is something that should be respected and relished as a way of encouraging us to vary our diets as the year goes by.

PACKAGING

These days our dustbins are awash with packaging materials – yoghurt pots, polythene bags, plastic bottles and polystyrene cups. These often unnecessary bi-products of the food we buy are expensive to produce and difficult to dispose of. As a consequence, bags, boxes, packets and wrappers (often non-biodegradable and sometimes actively harmful) are littering streets, clogging up landfill sites and polluting the environment. Reducing the amount of packaging – and thereby the amount of waste – in the home is a top priority. Here are some tips to help you do it:

- Avoid overpackaged food as much as you can. Instead of opting for prepacked vegetables and fruit, buy them loose; reduce the amount of ready-meals you buy; choose large bags of biscuits or crisps, for example, rather than lots of little ones.
- Reuse packaging. Fruit trays and yoghurt pots make good children's painting accessories, for example.
- Sort your rubbish (don't throw everything in the bin together) and recycle what you can – cardboard, glass and some plastics (call the manufacturer if you are not sure how to go about it).

IT IS WELL WORTH PAYING THAT LITTLE BIT EXTRA FOR HIGH-QUALITY, NATURALLY GROWN PRODUCE. GOOD FOOD, SIMPLY PREPARED, CAN'T BE BETTERED.

THE HEALTH ISSUE

Organic produce should taste better and may contain more vitamins and trace elements than conventionally produced food, but it is only as healthy as you choose to make it. Organic cakes and puddings, for example, may be more natural than their inorganic counterparts, but they will contain just as much sugar; organic chocolate may be purer and more delicious, but it will be just as fattening.

Organic foods are obviously far better for us than chemical-rich convenience foods and fast foods, but an organic diet – like any other diet – should include lots of fresh fruit and vegetables (governments worldwide, concerned about healthcare bills, are urging us to eat at least five portions a day). Eating traditional wholefoods is one way of ensuring a healthy diet, but if brown rice and beansprouts are not your thing, there are more exotic alternatives.

Ingredients from traditional Japanese cuisine – seaweed, soya and sushi, for example – are very nutritious and also very chic. While tofu and miso used to be bought only by die-hard health-foodies in the West, they have now hit the high street in a big way and sushi bars have become a firm favourite with style-conscious urbanites. High in protein and low in fat, sushi has to be one of the healthiest (and prettiest) fast foods around and it is a very good option for eco eating just as long as the fish hasn't been farmed and comes from a sustainable source.

Renée Elliott's favourite salad
(Renée Elliott is the founder of Planet Organic food store in London)

INGREDIENTS (all organic, of course)

Rocket, torn into small pieces

Cherry tomatoes cut into halves

Quartered, roasted artichoke hearts

Cucumber, sliced into delicate semicircles

Lightly roasted sunflower seeds

Grated Parmesan cheese

Olive oil and balsamic vinegar

Toss together for a delicious dish, full of healthy vitamins.

EATING

Nigella Lawson's pavlova (Nigella Lawson is a London-based food writer)

4 large organic **egg whites**

250 g (7 oz) organic **cane sugar**

2 tsps organic **cornflour** (Rapunzel maize starch is available in health food shops)

1 tsp organic **cider vinegar**

300 g (10 oz) (a couple of punnets) organic **redcurrants**

juice of 1 organic **orange**

4 tbsps organic **cane sugar**

400 ml (14 fl oz) organic **double cream**   Serves 6–8

Preheat the oven to 180°C/350°F/gas mark 4. Line a baking tray with baking parchment and – if you like things neat – draw a circle 20–23 cm (8–9 ¼ in) diameter, around a cake tin.

Whisk the egg whites until satiny peaks form, then beat in the sugar, a spoonful at a time, until the meringue is stiff and shiny. Sprinkle the cornflour and cider vinegar over the meringue and fold in gently. Mound onto the baking parchment, using a rubber spatula to smooth the top and flatten the sides. Put in the oven and immediately reduce the heat to 150°C/300°F/gas mark 2 and bake for one hour. Turn off the oven but leave the meringue inside until it has cooled. I often do this last thing at night and leave it in the oven until the next morning. If you want to make the base in advance, keep it, cooled, in a cake-sized Tupperware box.

About an hour before you want to assemble the pavlova, take most of the redcurrants off their stems and put them in a bowl to steep with the orange juice and two tablespoons of the sugar. After they've had their macerating time, beat the cream until it's thick, but still soft. Invert the meringue onto a flat plate, so that the crisp base is at the bottom. Onto its soft top, smear the whipped cream, and arrange the redcurrants, leaving some small, straggly lengths of fruit on their stem, letting them fall over the sides. Pour the juices from the fruit into a saucepan and add the other two tablespoons of sugar. Boil down until it becomes a coral-coloured syrup, and then, when cool, drizzle over the glassy berries.

If redcurrants elude you, use raspberries or strawberries instead. If you are going for the strawberry option, halve the fruits and steep them in a little sugar and a tablespoon of organic balsamic vinegar for an hour or so, before piling them on top of the whipped cream. Then boil down the fruity, vinegary juices to give you a little syrup to drizzle over the top.

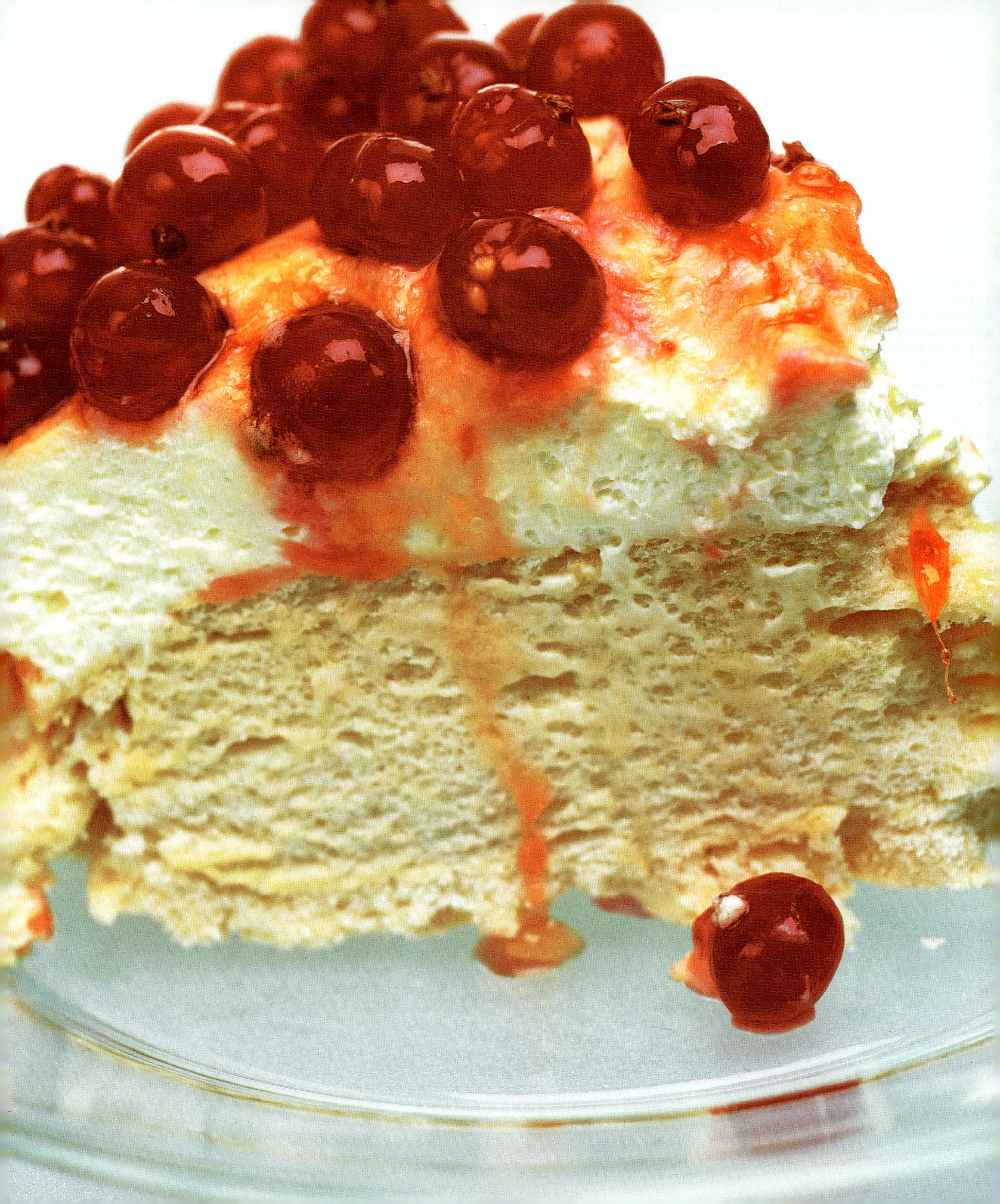

the drink

With the wide range of enticing natural health drinks on offer – including luscious smoothies, mouthwatering juices and energy-giving herbal tonics – there is no longer any reason to stick to stress-inducing coffee and sweetener-filled sodas, so think before you drink.

Most of us do not drink anything like enough to maintain healthy levels of fluid in our bodies, and what we do consume often does us and the environment more harm than good. These days, however, with the wide range of enticing natural health drinks on offer – including luscious smoothies, mouthwatering juices and energy-giving herbal tonics – there is no longer any reason to stick to stress-inducing coffee and sweetener-filled sodas, so think before you drink.

JUICE

We all know that vegetables are good for you, but why eat what you can drink? Carrots, celery, beetroot and greens – food we traditionally ate on a plate is being served up in liquid form on many an urban high street. Juice bars are the latest thing in the fast food business and, judging by their success, they are doing for health food what Birkenstock has done for clogs – making it trendy.

Juice, according to the nutrition experts, is raw energy and the purest form of food you can get. With each vegetable or fruit offering a different complex of life-enhancing nutrients, you could live on this liquid fodder for months without suffering any dire consequences. Juice detoxifies the body and cleanses the system; it may help to reduce your risk of cancer; it also gives you high doses of minerals, vitamins and enzymes in readily consumable form. And this is the point. While it would be difficult to eat six to eight carrots, say, at one sitting, if you juice them and break down the fibre, you can drink them with ease in an average-sized tumbler.

Buying from juice bars can be expensive, so why not make your own at home using a juicer or blender? Experiment with different combinations of fruits, vegetables and even grasses, but before you start, make sure you do not include the following, which can be toxic:

- Apple seeds (although lemon, lime, grape and melon pips are fine).
- Carrot and rhubarb greens.
- Orange and grapefruit skins (although the pith is very nutritious).
- Kiwi and papaya skins.
- Any fruit stones.

TAP INTO THE TREND FOR TURNING FRUITS, VEGETABLES AND HERBS INTO SMOOTHIES AND JUICES. YOU WON'T JUST BE IN VOGUE BUT IN BRILLIANT HEALTH, TOO.

energy boost

apple kick

(from Renée Elliott)
5–6 organic apples, unpeeled, quartered, cored and chopped
small piece of fresh organic ginger root
½ organic lemon, deseeded and chopped

Juice the ingredients together, pour into a glass and drink.

power boost

1 tart organic apple, unpeeled, quartered, cored and chopped
3–5 organic carrots, scrubbed, trimmed and chopped
2 stalks of organic kale, stems removed, washed and chopped

Juice the ingredients together, pour into a glass and drink immediately, but at least 15 minutes before eating a meal. This drink may be the colour of your lawn, but it's pleasant tasting, loaded with nutrients and packed with power.

pick-me-up smoothie

enticer

(from Russ Tice)
1 raw organic beetroot, scrubbed, trimmed and chopped
several sprigs of fresh parsley
1 small to medium apple, unpeeled, quartered, cored and chopped
several sprigs of wheatgrass (optional)
2 tablespoons raw honey (optional)
ice or water for desired consistency

Place all the ingredients in a blender and process at the highest speed for 3 minutes. Pour into a glass and drink. This quick and easy juice will cleanse your liver, purge toxins and rejuvenate you!

sparkling memory

(from Cherie Calbom)
4–5 organic carrots, scrubbed, trimmed and chopped
3 stalks of organic celery, with leaves if liked, washed and chopped
¼ head small organic cabbage, cut into sections to fit your juicer and washed
¼ organic lemon, unpeeled (optional)

This drink is good for improving the memory and is surprisingly delicious, with a slightly 'nutty' flavour. It is also especially rich in choline, one of the B vitamins that increases acetylcholine, a substance that is the message carrier of the brain.

Juice together the carrots, celery and cabbage; add the lemon if using. Stir well and drink chilled or at room temperature.

purity

WHEATGRASS

Strong, bitter but amazingly good for you, wheatgrass (the young wheat plant) has become the favourite tipple of stressed-out city slickers and many other health-conscious drinkers besides. Dark, potent and grassy in flavour, it takes some getting used to but can't be bettered for nutritional value. Wheatgrass contains most of the vitamins and minerals needed for human maintenance; its high chlorophyll content acts as a 'magnet' in drawing out toxins from the body; and just 50 g (2 oz) of fresh wheatgrass juice is said to have the equivalent nutritional value of around 2 kg (4 lb) of organic green vegetables. Drink a shot of it to boost your body or use it to cleanse your skin, heal cuts and bruises, clear blocked sinuses, stimulate circulation or perk up lacklustre hair.

MILK

Sadly, this traditional staple of our diet is no longer quite as natural and wholesome as it once was. Conventionally reared dairy cows are routinely given hormones to increase their yields, and these can't help but be passed on to us in their milk. While the long-term effects of ingesting such hormones are not yet clear, some experts think it probable that there is a correlation between their use and the growing incidence of hormone-related cancers. At this stage, choosing to buy organic milk and, by extension, other dairy produce such as yoghurt, cream and cheese, seems to be the only sensible option.

WATER

Tap water, too, is not as pure as it should be. Much of it has become contaminated with chlorine, metals, nitrates and pesticides, which are bad for both you and the environment. Unfortunately, the answer does not lie with bottled water, which is far more expensive than metered tap water and not necessarily any purer. Instead, invest in a water filter, available from most good eco suppliers, which will remove pollutants and improve the taste of your water. It should also help to soften water and reduce the build-up of limescale in your kettle. A water-filtering jug is the cheapest option, but tap filters and on-line filters that fit under the sink are also available.

OPPOSITE: ONCE YOUR WATER IS PURE, MAKE SURE YOUR TUMBLERS ARE, TOO. BANISH GARISH PLASTIC BEAKERS IN FAVOUR OF COOL RECYCLED GLASSES AND DRINK TO THE HEALTH OF THE PLANET.

BELOW: GREEN TEA, MADE FROM THE NATURAL DRIED LEAVES OF THE TEA PLANT, HAS BEEN DRUNK FOR CENTURIES, BUT NOT JUST FOR PLEASURE. FAMED WORLDWIDE FOR ITS MEDICINAL PROPERTIES, IT IS SAID TO HELP TO PREVENT CANCER, CONTROL HIGH BLOOD PRESSURE AND EVEN SUPPRESS THE SIGNS OF AGEING.

lounging

The organic look for the living room is all the rage at the moment – grass cloth wallpaper, bamboo flooring, rattan furniture and fabric strewn with leaves. Nature is suddenly hip in the home again, and not for the first time. At the end of the nineteenth century, the artists and artisans of the Art Nouveau school took it as a starting point for their swirling botanical designs and decorations; in the 1950s and 1960s, Space Age designers used natural forms as inspiration for their futuristic furniture and other objects; in the 1990s nature came into the home literally with driftwood furniture, rush matting and twiggy accessories. Nature, albeit in various forms, has never been out of fashion for long and now the time is ripe for a living-room look which is eco-friendly and ultra chic.

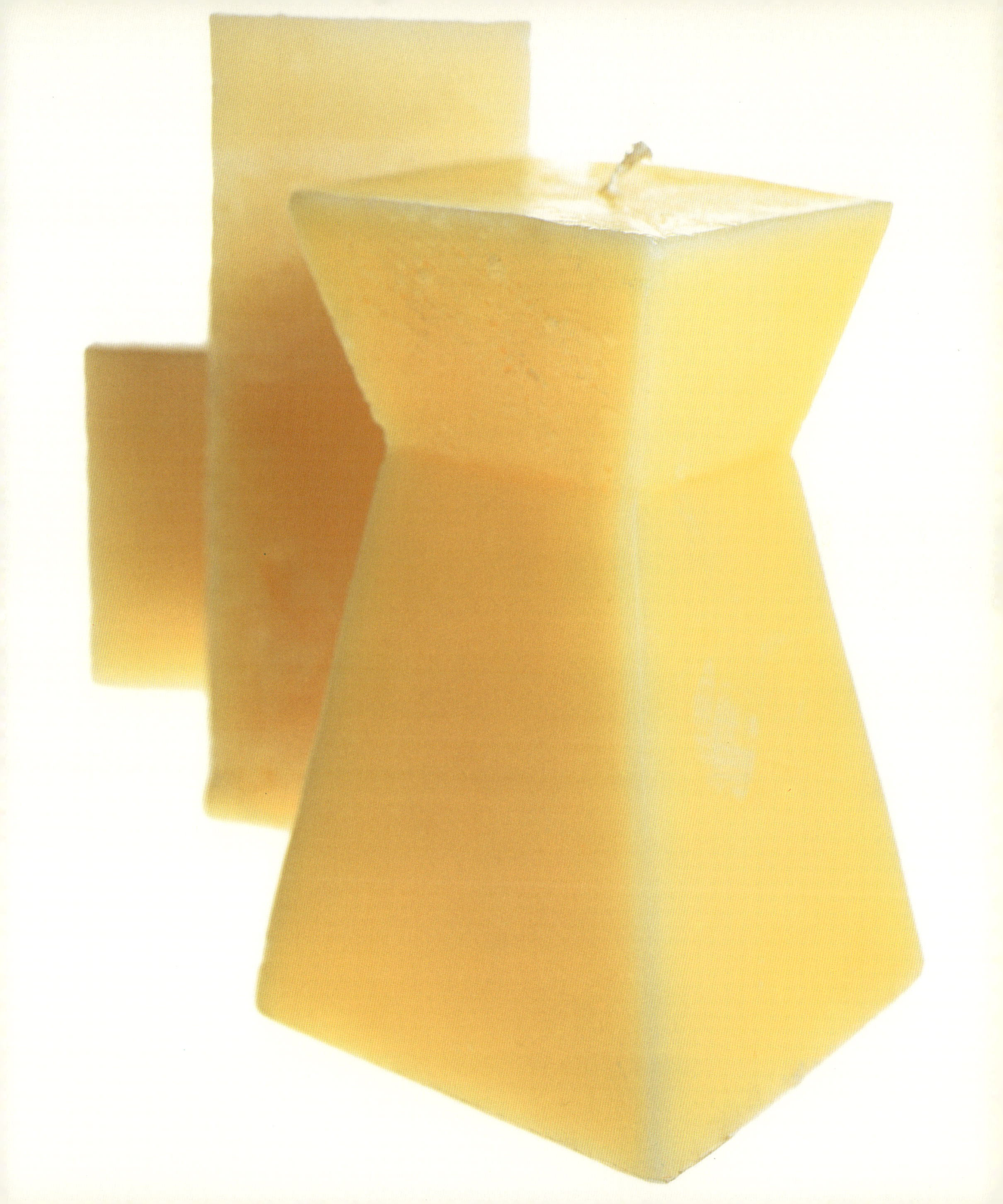

the living space

Organic shapes are popular in the home because they are soft and easy on the eye. Fluid and comfortable, they are a natural counterpoint to the man-made rectilinear feel of most conventional interiors.

Organic shapes are popular in the home because they are soft and easy on the eye. Fluid and comfortable, they are a natural counterpoint to the man-made rectilinear feel of most conventional interiors. But an eco aesthetic isn't necessarily eco-friendly. A sinuous, stem-shaped chair may look in tune with nature but, if it is made of plastic, it will work against it. Sisal matting may seem the most natural of floor coverings but, if it is backed with a synthetic material, it can do as much harm to the environment – and to you – as any artificial alternative.

BELOW: IN KEEPING WITH THE MODERN TAKE ON ORGANIC LIVING, THIS LOFT SPACE IN NEW YORK WAS FILLED ENTIRELY WITH RECYCLED THINGS, BUT LOOKS THE HEIGHT OF CONTEMPORARY URBAN COOL.

design
When you come to kit out your living room, do a bit of research. Find out exactly what the materials comprise – some so-called natural products hide chemical components – and choose the greenest things you can. This doesn't mean you have to fill your living space with bare pine and hessian: the eco home today can embrace everything from industrial salvage to recycled plastic and give you a look as chic, urban and sophisticated as any conventional scheme.

walls
Rough textures and natural motifs such as leaves, grasses, pebbles or flowers will give your walls cutting-edge natural looks, but be sure that whatever coverings you choose will give them eco credentials, too.

WALLPAPER
There are so many papers to choose from these days, it is easy to find one that is both funky and eco-friendly. Avoid those with waterproof finishes, such as vinyl, which may give off harmful vapours and which don't allow moisture to evaporate; in humid or damp areas like a kitchen or bathroom this can be a particular problem. Alternatively, don't buy conventional wallpaper at all; think of different eco-friendly coverings for your walls, such as old maps or even recycled newspaper. Whatever you choose, stick it to the wall with organic glue, as the fungicides and chemical adhesives used in most wallpaper pastes can irritate the skin.

AN ECO-FRIENDLY LIVING ROOM NEEDN'T BE BROWN OR EARTHY, TODAY THE GREEN LOOK CAN ENCOMPASS EVERYTHING FROM SECOND-HAND FURNITURE TO INDUSTRIAL SALVAGE.

LOUNGING 39

PAINTING YOUR WALLS WITH THE
PLANET IN MIND DOESN'T MEAN
YOU HAVE TO STICK TO EARTHY
COLOURS. ORGANIC PAINTS CAN
COME IN BRILLIANT TONES AND
EVEN FUNKY FINISHES CAN BE
ECO-FRIENDLY. THESE CORD
AND DENIM WATER-BASED PAINT
EFFECTS PRODUCED BY BENETTON
WILL BRING YOUR WALLS RIGHT
UP TO DATE WITH MINIMAL HARM
TO THE ENVIRONMENT.

FABRICS

Natural fabrics will add instant texture to your walls and, if thick enough, they will provide more insulation than paper. Woollen felt, which is made simply by pressing and injecting wool with steam, is one of the most fashionable and most eco-friendly. 'It is one of the greenest engineered textiles known to man,' says a representative from the British Felt Company. 'Bury it in the ground and it will rot naturally, and fertilize your plants at the same time.' (This is because when decomposing it gives off nitrous oxides which are natural fertilizers.) Try to avoid synthetic fibres and any fabric with a plastic backing. (For more on fabrics, see 'Sleeping & Dressing', page 108.)

CORK

Cork tiles used to be the butt of every interior design joke but this 1970s' favourite is now at the top of every style-conscious consumer's shopping list. Brilliant for sound and heat insulation, cork is one of the most eco-friendly and practical materials for the home, and it won't rot or go mouldy. Made from the outer bark of the cork oak tree, it is easily sustainable since the bark can be harvested every eight to ten years without damaging the tree. Just make sure you avoid tiles with a plastic backing and use natural glue to fix them in place.

WOOD VENEERS

For a pukka modern finish, little can beat a wood veneer, but choose your timber carefully. Avoid endangered tropical hardwood veneers (see page 131) and choose wood from a sustainable source. If the veneer is being supported by a plywood or chipboard base, make sure this has been properly sealed to avoid offgassing (see page 15), or that it is a low-emission or ecological variety, which uses polyurethane rather than formaldehyde binder. In addition, avoid chemical adhesives.

IF IN DOUBT, FAKE IT
If you cannot find out the provenance of a veneer, why not fake the timber look with wood-effect wallpaper, which is the height of fashion and a lot cheaper, too?

PAINT
Conventional paints are extremely polluting and, considering how extensive our use of them is in the home, it is high time we switched to organic alternatives.

POLLUTING PAINTS
Most shop-bought paints are made from petrochemical derivatives which are bad not only for the environment but for our health, too. Many synthetic solvents, which are used to make paint flow easily, are classified as carcinogenic; vinyl resins such as those found in conventional emulsion wall paints can damage the lungs, liver and blood, and cause skin irritation. Decorators who use these paints are prone to suffer from dermatitis, bronchitis and asthma, or even damage to the nervous system. In Denmark, 'Painters Dementia' is a recognized industrial disease.

Many paint manufacturers are now promoting water-based paints as an alternative to their toxic ranges, but these are not necessarily as eco-friendly as they seem. As UK eco builders merchant, Construction Resources, says: 'These actually contain more chemicals than the oil-based paints they are intended to replace and several of their components evaporate for a long time after painting and may affect human physiology.' The indoor environment is now thought to be up to ten times more polluted than the outdoor environment (see information on sick building syndrome, page 69) and the fact that up to 90 per cent of internal surfaces are covered with petrochemical paints must be a contributing factor.

THE NATURAL ALTERNATIVE
The only really safe and eco-friendly option is to choose natural paints when you come to decorate your home. These are made from linseed oil – produced by crushing seeds from the fully renewable crop, flax – which is blended with other natural oils, resins and pigments, all of which are either renewable or in plentiful supply. Organic paints are microporous (so they shouldn't flake) and waterproof. Both organic emulsions and gloss paints are available, and although they may take a little longer to dry than conventional varieties, they are easy to use, should not crack and, best of all, won't pollute indoor air.

Traditional paints, such as distemper or casein milk paint, also contain no synthetic ingredients and will give you a classic, matt finish. Distemper, however, does wash off when it comes in contact with water, so if you want a water-resistant finish, you will need to use an oil-based version.

As for colour, you are not restricted to a palette of earthy browns and sludgy greens. Although your choice won't be as great as for the petrochemical paints, intensely coloured vegetable and mineral pigments (such as ultramarine or oxide yellow) are available. Many suppliers offer both ready-made colours and paint with separate pigment sachets, so that you can mix a colour yourself to whatever strength you desire.

VARNISHES
Before you apply varnish, consider first whether you really need it. Good-quality wooden surfaces may look far better if they are left natural or just given a simple wax finish. If you decide, though, that a sleek and shiny surface is a must, avoid synthetic varnishes, which may contain solvents and traces of lead.

Natural alternatives to varnish include shellac, a pure resin with good sealing properties, and 'lazur', a biodegradable and microporous varnish made from tree and plant oils, which should be available from organic paint suppliers.

STRAIGHT LINES WERE BANNED
IN THIS CURVY ORGANIC PAD
DESIGNED BY ARCHITECT JAVIER
SENOSIAIN AGUILAR IN A SUBURB
OF MEXICO CITY. OUTSIDE ITS
GRASS-COVERED ROOF ECHOES
THE SHAPE OF THE SURROUNDING
HILLSIDE; INSIDE BRILLIANT COLOUR
AND FREE-FORM SHAPES MAKE IT
LOOK MORE LIKE A PSYCHEDELIC
RABBIT WARREN THAN A HUMAN
LIVING SPACE.

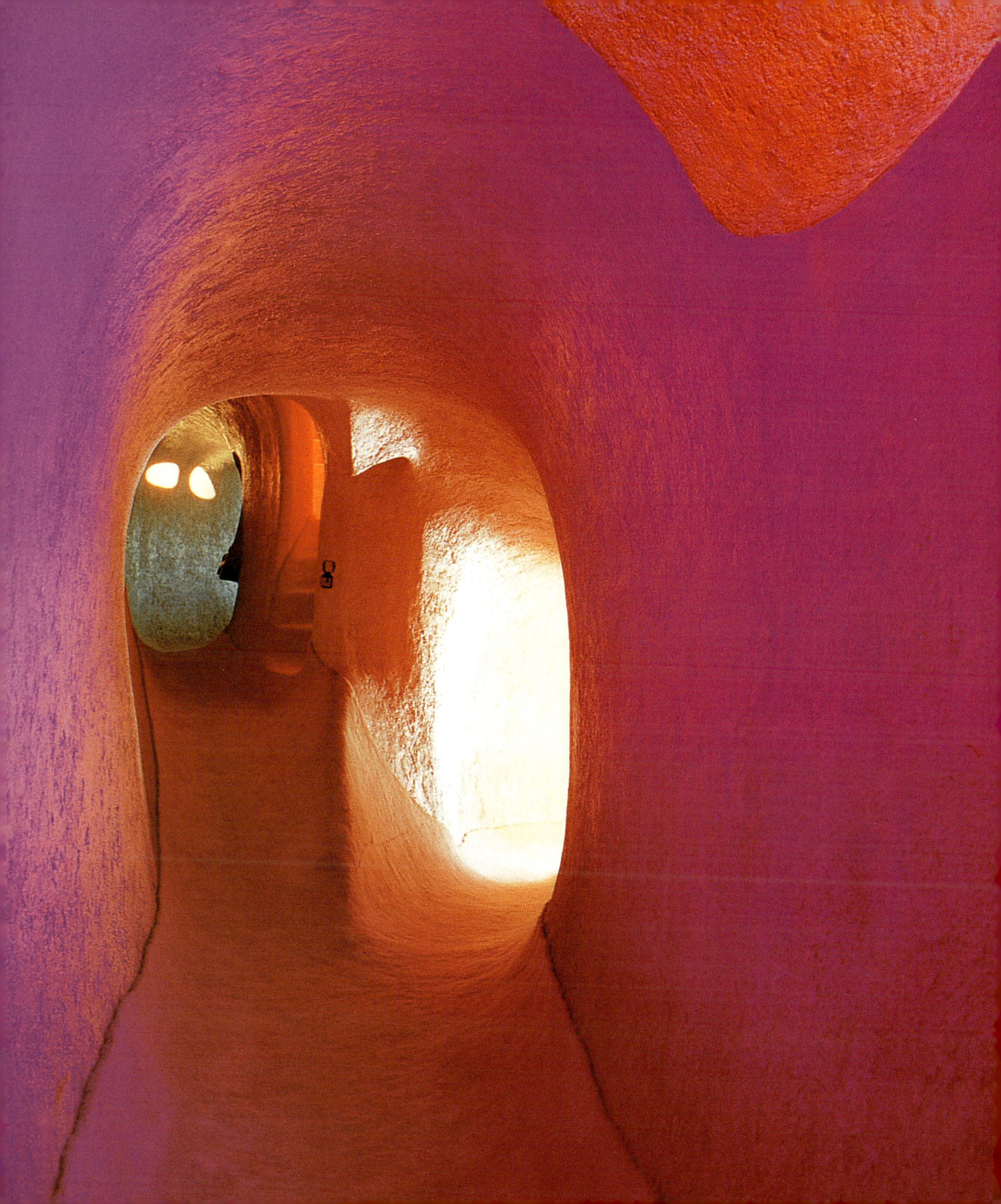

floors

We choose flooring for comfort and durability as well as for looks, but how many of us consider how eco-friendly a material is before we buy it? Given the enormous variety of flooring options on offer, it is easy to choose a material that looks good and won't harm our health or that of the planet. (See page 12 for information on stone and ceramic floors.)

WOOD AND TIMBER PRODUCTS

Natural, versatile, warm and durable, solid wood is the ideal material for flooring and it can be an eco option if it comes from a sustainable source (see page 131) or is salvaged. If you are buying new, look for a label from The Forest Stewardship Council (FSC), an international body that accredits sustainable timber; contact Friends of the Earth for information or find out the exact provenance of the wood from the supplier.

As a rule of thumb, avoid tropical hardwoods, which are particularly endangered, or source these from a reclaimed timber yard. Alternatively, use American or European temperate hardwoods, such as maple or elm, both of which are perfect for flooring, or softwoods, which can be just as durable (the term 'softwood' applies to the cell structure of the trees, not to the strength of the wood). Many of these work well underfoot (larch, hemlock or spruce, for example) but, due to overuse, some softwoods are also becoming scarce. The solution is to buy all your timber from managed sources if you can. Also, check with your supplier whether the wood you choose has come into contact with pesticides; if it has, seal it with a natural varnish (see page 41).

LAMINATES AND PLYWOODS

These are far cheaper than solid wood and, since they use less timber for the same visual effect, could be considered more environmentally friendly. This is only true, however, if they have been manufactured without chemical ingredients. Make sure that whichever product you choose, it is formaldehyde-free or at least classified as 'low-emission' to avoid health problems – particularly if you are sensitive to chemicals. (See Plastics, plywoods and particleboards, page 15.)

CORK

This is a good option for both you and the environment (see page 40), and perfect for bathroom or kitchen floors.

LINOLEUM

Made of harvestable raw materials, such as powdered cork and linseed oil, linoleum scores highly on the eco-friendly hit list. Choose brands that use harmless natural pigments and those that are backed with jute rather than PVC, making them completely biodegradable; the drawback, though, is that this will limit their use to damp-free areas.

RUBBER

Tough, waterproof and flexible, rubber is brilliant for floors, but make sure you choose a natural rather than a synthetic variety. Demand for latex, the raw material extracted from the rubber tree, is already far outstripping supply, however, so rubber, too, needs to be used sparingly.

NATURAL FLOORING

Fast-growing bamboo is just the thing for a fashionable floor and is eco-friendly as long as it comes from a cultivated plantation (extensive harvesting of wild varieties can endanger the wildlife that feed off it). Try to avoid canes that have been treated with pesticides (dark flecks can be an indication of this); if you are not sure, seal with a natural varnish.

Seagrass, sisal and coir matting are marketed by manufacturers as the 'natural' alternative to conventional flooring, but this is often misleading. Although the materials themselves are natural and sustainable – sisal comes from the *Agave sisalana* and coir from the husk of the coconut – they are often dyed with synthetic dyes and backed with harmful and non-biodegradable synthetic latex. For a truly natural floor, opt for those backed with natural latex, jute or woollen felt.

CARPET

Carpet has a high comfort factor and is good for sound and heat insulation but, whether short pile or shag pile, it can come with an environmental cost. Synthetic carpets can emit a variety of harmful chemicals long after they have been laid and can cause static build-up, both of which have negative implications for health. Woven wool carpet may seem the obvious eco alternative, but many so-called 'natural' carpets have synthetic backing and contain synthetic dyes and toxic mothproofer, making them as environmentally damaging as their artificial relations. The only green option is to buy carpet that is guaranteed 100 per cent natural, so find out exactly what a carpet contains before you buy. Good ecological suppliers are on the increase and most should be able to offer truly natural carpet in a range of colours, weights and grades, and with a choice of backing (natural latex, jute or wool are the most common). Natural carpet may be a little more expensive now, but as demand increases, so prices should fall.

VINYL

Many floors these days are topped with vinyl (most commonly polyvinyl chloride or PVC) because it is flexible, waterproof and comes in countless colours and finishes. Despite its tempting versatility, it should be avoided if possible. It may cover up damp patches, but trapping moisture below the surface can encourage mould. Also, more significantly, it may release harmful vapours, especially in humid environments; it consumes vast amounts of energy during its production and it is not biodegradable.

THERE ARE COUNTLESS OPTIONS
FOR ECO FLOORS, FROM COARSE
COIR MATTING TO FUNKY FELT;
CORK TILES TO SMOOTH SALVAGED
WOOD. HOWEVER, SO THAT YOU
CAN BE TRULY ECO-FRIENDLY
UNDERFOOT, MAKE SURE BEFORE
YOU BUY THAT ANY SO-CALLED
NATURAL FLOOR COVERING
DOESN'T CONTAIN ANY HARMFUL
CHEMICALS (MANY DO) AND THAT
IT IS BACKED BY A MATERIAL
THAT IS ALSO 100 PER CENT
NATURAL. OFTEN THESE WILL COST
NO MORE THAN THE SYNTHETIC
VERSIONS AND WILL BE BETTER FOR
BOTH YOU AND THE ENVIRONMENT.

furniture & furnishings

In our consumer-led society we are used to buying furniture for our home whenever we feel like it, and fashion feeds our belief that we won't be stylish until we have thrown out the old and brought in the new. Not only is this throwaway philosophy damaging to the environment, it is also based on a false concept. Style is not dependent on the latest media must-haves but on what we do with whatever we have. The old, salvaged and second-hand can give us a look that is just as cutting-edge and far less costly to both us and the environment.

So don't rush to the nearest shopping centre in search of a new sofa or a new table, consider alternative and more eco-friendly ways of buying furniture first. Visit a salvage yard or auction house for classic old pieces; seek out designers who work with recycled or reappropriated materials or shops that specialize in ex-commercial or industrial kit. If we approach the furnishing of our homes with an eco attitude, we can help to reduce the damaging impact of consumerism on the planet.

BIO FURNITURE

No, this is not the latest GM experiment, but a term used to describe furniture that is kind to the environment and to us. As David Pearson says in *The New Natural House Book*: 'To be truly healthy all furniture must ... promote good posture and relaxation – firm support, correct height and the right body position.' This preoccupation with ergonomics is nothing new. In 1940 the Museum of Modern Art in New York ran a competition for the best organic design in home furnishings, resulting in a series of highly progressive shapely designs, which are still classics today (the Organic Armchair by Eero

BRILLIANTLY ERGONOMIC, MID-CENTURY DESIGNS SUCH AS ARNE JACOBSEN'S EGG CHAIR (LEFT), AND EERO SAARINEN'S TULIP CHAIRS (RIGHT) WILL GIVE YOU ORGANIC LOOKS IN AN INSTANT, BUT THEY AREN'T ALWAYS QUITE AS ECO-FRIENDLY AS THEY SEEM.

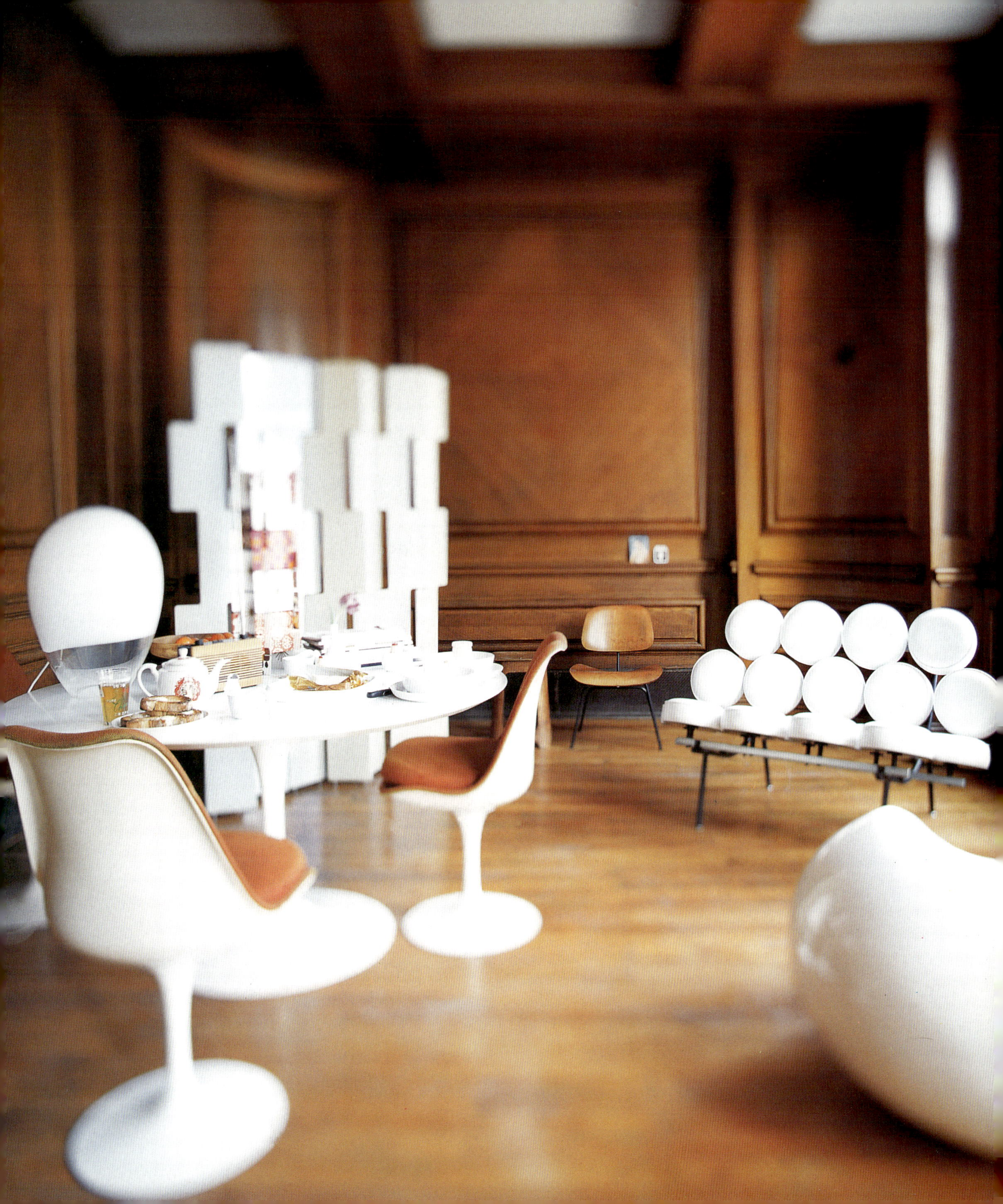

FOR THE ULTIMATE ECO LIVING ROOM, COMBINE CURVY ERGONOMIC FURNITURE WITH ACCESSORIES IN ORGANIC SHAPES AND RECYCLED OR REAPPROPRIATED MATERIALS. THE LAMP (TOP RIGHT) BY UK DESIGN TEAM JAM, FOR EXAMPLE, WAS MADE USING DISCARDED STRIPS OF FILM.

Saarinen and Charles Eames, for example). Although eco-friendly in shape, not all of these fashionable mid-century pieces are eco-friendly in substance – many were made with 'new' materials such as plastic and plywood. Eco puritans would do better to choose more recent ergonomic designs in wholly 'natural' materials.

THE GOODIES

The most eco-friendly furniture is that which has had the least done to it – and thus used up little energy in the making – so simple pieces made from natural materials come out top on the eco hit list. If you are sitting on untreated timber chairs and eating from a woven cane table, your eco credentials will be unquestionable, as long as all the materials come from sustainable sources and have not been treated with chemical pesticides, of course. But you don't have to opt for a raw and rugged look; these days it's easy to find sleek wooden and rattan furniture in modern shapes.

METALS AND GLASS

The favourite materials of the modern movement will give you a cool contemporary look that is reasonably green. Although more processed than organic materials, both metal and glass are non-toxic and the raw materials from which they are derived are fairly abundant, although zinc, lead, tin and tungsten are becoming scarce. Also, both metal and glass can be effectively recycled with little visible difference in quality – if you dispose of them conscientiously, that is.

While the modernists chose to accentuate the hardness of these materials with clean-lined rectilinear furniture, today's designers are more inventive, manipulating metals and glass into surprisingly fluid forms that will give you organic looks, too.

There is one problem with metal furniture, however. Some experts believe it can disturb natural electromagnetic fields (EMFs), exposure to which can cause adverse health reactions. Feng shui aficionados advise against metal beds for this reason and if this is something that worries you, opt for wood instead.

THE BADDIES

The invention of plastic and the discovery of injection moulding in the 1960s heralded a new age of furniture design. Suddenly our homes could be filled cheaply with chairs and tables in all manner of shapes, textures and colours. Many of the first plastic products came in organic forms (Verner Panton's famous stacking chair, for example), but their arrival signalled a downturn in the health of the planet and the home. Plastics consume vast amounts of energy during their production; most are non-biodegradable, few are recyclable and some can even give off harmful vapours when warm (see page 15).

urban eco

No longer the preserve of whimsical do-gooders, effective recycling of all our goods is now a global necessity if we are to retain at least some of the earth's already depleted natural resources and begin to reduce the vast amount of global waste.

Despite its catalogue of sins, plastics have continued to proliferate in the design world and they appear in many guises. As well as the evidently synthetic furniture – the PVC inflatable chair, for example, or the polypropylene lamp base – there are plastics in upholstery foam (although the very dangerous polyurethane foam is banned in most countries these days), in cushion pads, synthetic fabrics, laminated boards, adhesives, electrical fittings and so on. Today it would be virtually impossible to furnish your home without plastics. All you can do is try to limit their use or, if you want that 1960s look, consider using recycled or reappropriated plastic products, which are relatively green.

(For information on the other baddies, see Plastics, plywoods and particleboards, page 15.)

BELOW: TODAY'S GREEN LOOK CAN BE GROOVY AND URBAN, COMBINING ECO ELEMENTS WITH EX-FACTORY FITTINGS AND CITY SALVAGE.

RECYCLE, REUSE

This must be the mantra of the twenty-first century. No longer the preserve of whimsical do-gooders, effective recycling of all our goods is now a global necessity if we are to retain at least some of the earth's already depleted natural resources and begin to reduce the vast amount of global waste (see Rubbish, page 19).

While many of us may take bottles to a bottle bank or old clothes to a charity shop, far fewer of us think of recycling when it comes to furniture. We may buy second-hand and salvaged pieces – which is helpful in as much as it reduces the demand for new products – but this is recycling more by accident than design. If we are serious about environmental issues, we must increase our quota of green furniture. As the brochure from 'Recycling', a recent British touring exhibition, cited: 'Sustainable consumers need to develop an aesthetic taste for the raw, the partially cooked and the reheated; they need to appreciate the inherent quality in something that was waste.' The good news is, this doesn't mean we have to give up on style.

Using furniture made from totally recycled materials is a way of kitting out your home with a conscience. 'Recycling saves energy to such an extent that secondary aluminium, for example, consumes only 5 per cent of the energy used to extract and process primary ore,' says David Pearson in *The New Natural House Book*; and the principle applies to many other materials, too. Even certain plastics can be effectively recycled and used to make funky modern furniture (see page 14).

LOUNGING 51

ABOVE: BRING A COOL, MODERN EDGE TO A GREEN SCHEME BY INCLUDING CAST-OFFS FROM THE BUILDERS YARD IN THE INTERIOR MIX. STACKED-UP BREEZE BLOCKS, FOR EXAMPLE, WILL MAKE A FUNKY AND FUNCTIONAL ROOM DIVIDER.

OPPOSITE: SIMPLE BAMBOO MATS AND PAPYRUS PLANTS ADD A NATURAL TOUCH TO A CITY LOFT.

URBAN ECO

The detritus of the building industry – breeze blocks, scaffolding poles, concrete slabs and the like – would once have been discarded, but these items are now considered 'chicer' than chic. This is due, in part, to the trend for loft-living, with ex-industrial spaces being converted into fashionable apartments in cities all over the world. Look out for utilitarian ex-factory or commercial fittings – salvaged iron radiators, storage racks on wheels, metal filing cabinets and old office swivel chairs, for example – which will give your home good eco credentials and add a bit of urban kudos to any wholesome green scheme.

CREATIVE SALVAGE

This phrase was coined to describe the work of a stable of designers in the mid-1980s, who created funky and functional objects out of salvage. Tom Dixon – now creative director of Habitat UK – was a renowned exponent, famous for making seats out of traffic bollards, for example. Today, the practice continues with many a cutting-edge, eco-conscious designer creating covetable objects from reappropriated and waste products. Look out for sardine-tin drawers (Michael Marriott), yardstick tables (Jane Atfield) and bowls made out of washing-machine fronts (One Foot Taller). Never has old scrap looked so good.

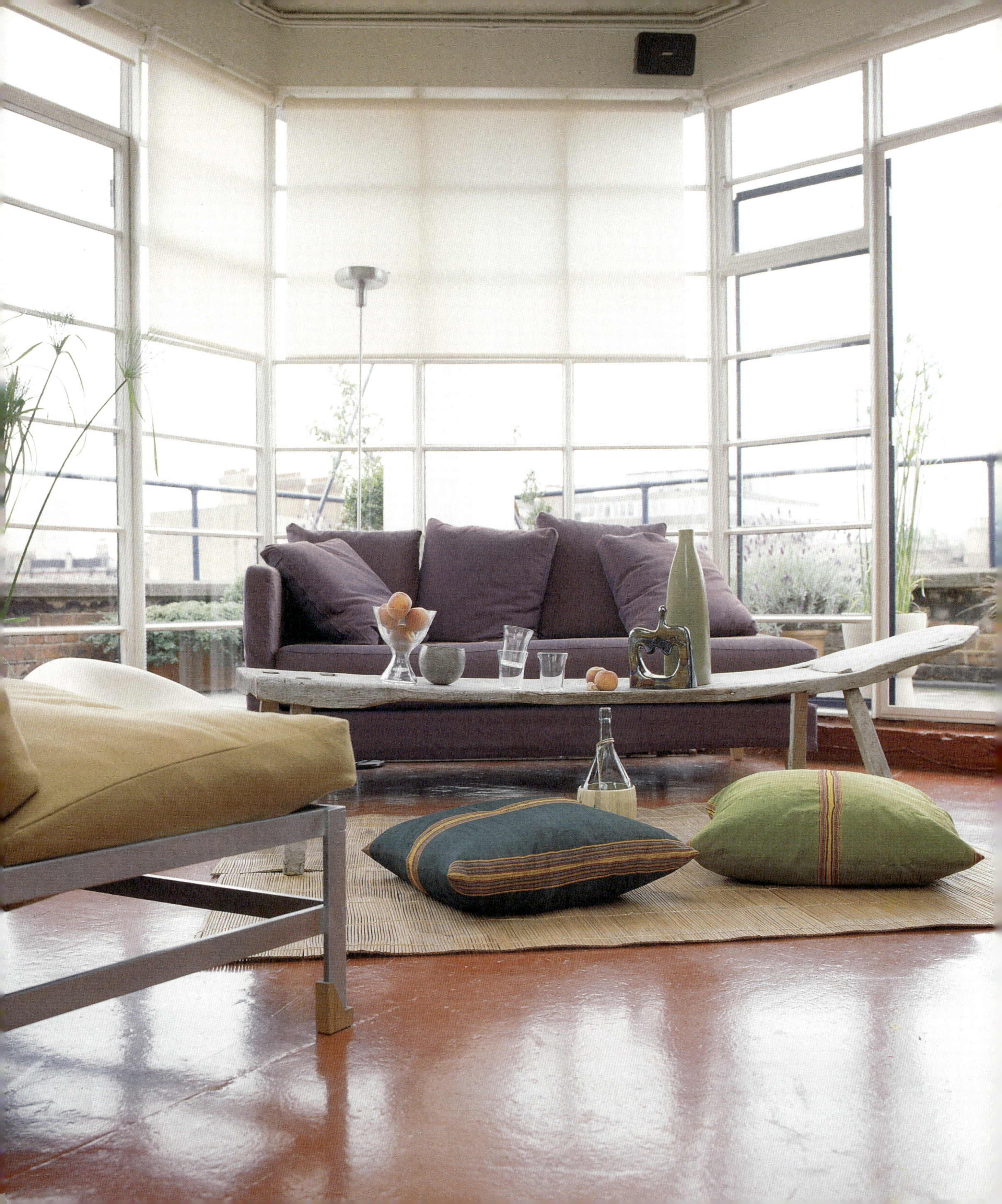

Thanks to stylish interiors magazines, natural textures – such as raw wood or rough ceramic – and organic shapes are back in fashion, so it is easy to make your home trendy and green. Get the look, as here, with shapely wooden furniture, natural fabrics and sculptural accessories.

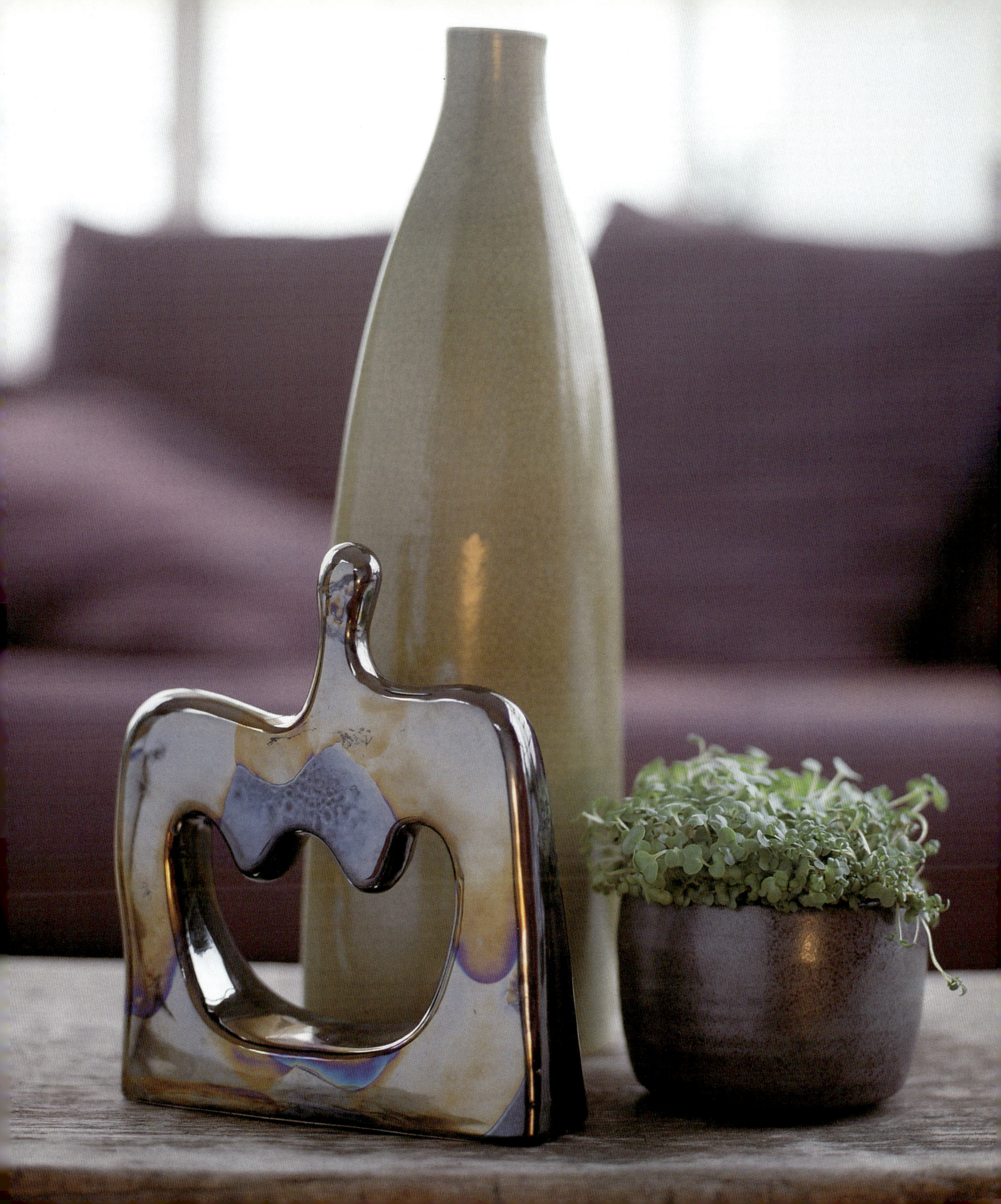

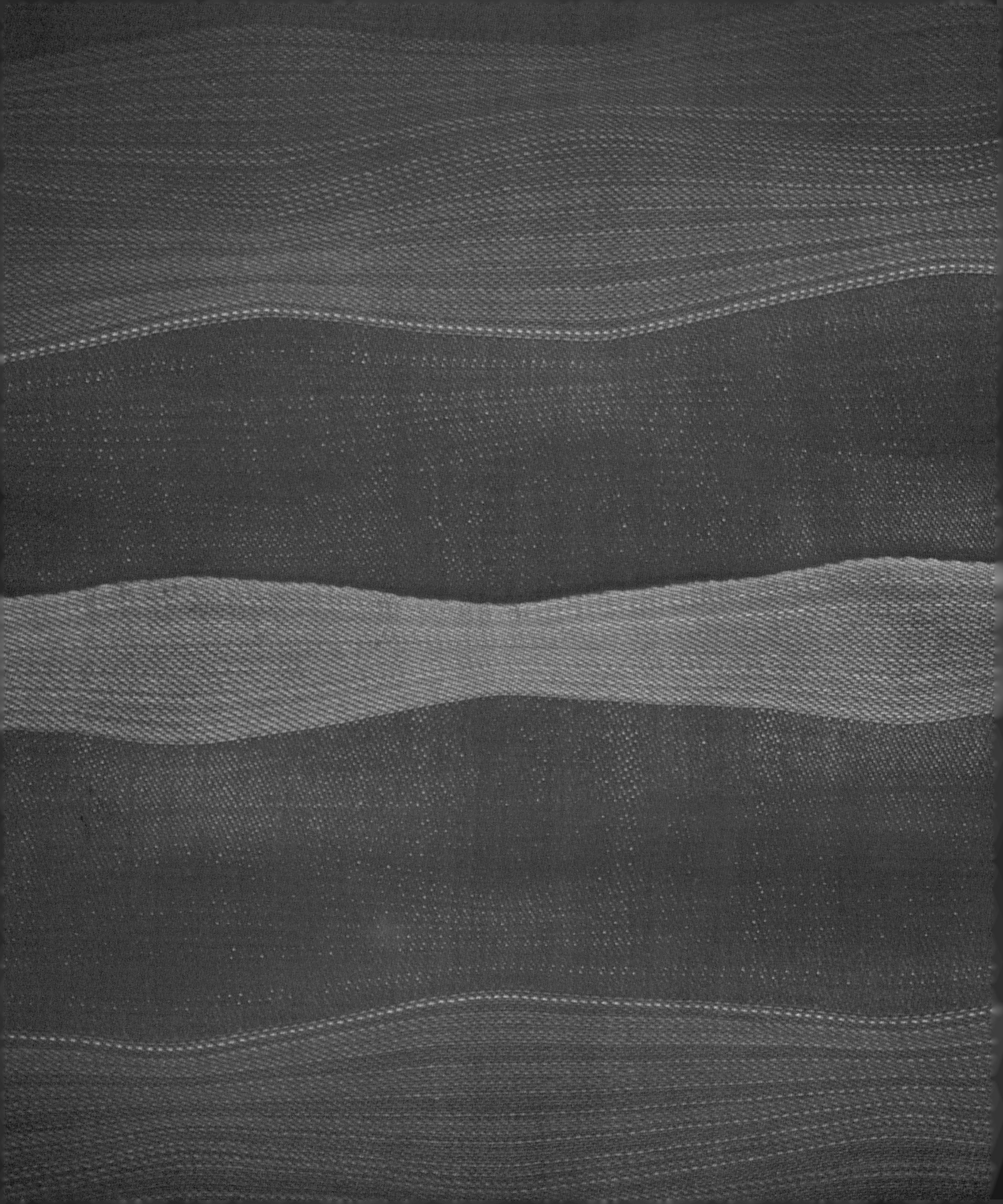

ECO-FRIENDLY FURNISHINGS

It is easy to get the green look with your furnishings – leafy design loose covers, coarsely textured curtains, pebble-printed cushions, among others – but natural patterns may camouflage unnatural fibres. Many fabrics in the home nowadays contain synthetics and while they may look good, the majority are produced from non-renewable resources, consume vast amounts of energy in their production and are not biodegradable.

The alternative is to opt for natural fabrics, but these may not be as 'natural' as they seem. Cotton, for example, is generally sprayed very heavily with pesticides while it is growing and then bleached and treated before being dyed (often with synthetic dyes). Linen, too, is bleached with chemicals today (it used to be left outside to fade naturally in the sun) and also habitually dyed with synthetics. Both are generally treated with fire-retardant finishes which can contain a harmful formaldehyde compound.

The solution to this problem is to buy 'organic' cottons, unbleached linen or raw silk – classic go-anywhere fabrics which make great curtains or chair covers (though note that any upholstered furniture bought from a shop will probably contain a fireproof element). These fabrics may be harder to find and a little more expensive than the rest, but it's worth paying a bit extra for truly natural materials.

If you are after a more textured finish, try hessian (made from sustainable jute and hemp), canvas or wool – as long as it is 100 per cent natural (look for the official Woolmark label). Leather, too, is a good green option for upholstery if it is undyed and has been sourced without cruelty to animals. An added bonus with protein-based fibres (wool, leather and silk) is that they burn at much higher temperatures than the plant-based ones and in some countries can be sold untreated.

CRISP COTTON, COARSELY WOVEN HESSIAN, SUPER-SOFT WOOL – NATURAL FABRICS ARE BIG ON TEXTURE AND WILL GIVE YOUR HOME A SENSUAL AS WELL AS AN ECO-FRIENDLY TOUCH. KEEP THINGS PLAIN OR CHOOSE MORE DECORATIVE ONE-OFF TEXTILES, WHICH CAN BE THROWN OVER THE BACK OF A SOFA, HUNG UP AT THE WINDOW OR FRAMED ON THE WALL LIKE A PIECE OF ART. THESE HANDWOVEN DESIGNS ARE BY ANNE SELIM (LEFT) AND ZOE HOPE (RIGHT).

ACCESSORIES

The decorative details of your interior count just as much as the grand scheme, so choose accessories that will complement your eco living space. Organic, flowing shapes, natural textures and recycled materials are key: bulbous ceramic vases, curvy wooden candlesticks, baskets made of discarded plastic, industrial products, recycled paper or packaging.

The green look is very chic at the moment, so any natural accessory will give you instant style as well as adding a fashionable 'soul' element to your interior. And don't forget to bring a bit of living nature inside, too – a tray of wheatgrass on a table, perhaps, or a window box filled with home-grown herbs.

WINDOWS

An eco home should maximize sunlight and conserve heat, so think of imaginative and stylish ways to screen your windows which will satisfy both criteria. Here are some ideas:

- Curtains will keep in the heat effectively but they can consume vast amounts of costly fabric. Buy second-hand if you can or adapt existing material to fit your windows (an antique quilt, perhaps, or an Indian sari). Make sure, too, that curtains can be kept completely away from the windows during the day to let as much light as possible into the interior.
- Have two sets of curtains – thin ones in muslin or light cotton for summer and thick ones in wool or even fleece for winter – so you can switch them season by season.
- If you have giant windows, camouflage the lower part of them with a row of tall leafy plants: the ultimate green screen.
- If your home faces north and needs all the sunlight it can get, consider less permanent screening solutions – cane shutters or a bamboo screen, for example.

TOP LEFT AND OPPOSITE: LIGHT
AND AIRY, THIS CONVERTED STABLE
ON THE FRINGES OF CAPE TOWN
IS AN EFFECTIVE AND HEALTHY
MIX OF ELEMENTAL ARCHITECTURE,
INDUSTRIAL SALVAGE AND SIMPLE
CLASSIC FURNITURE.

LEFT: IF YOU LIKE THE LOOK BUT
CAN'T COPE WITH COWHIDE IN
YOUR HOME, OPT FOR FAKE
LEATHER INSTEAD, BUT MAKE SURE
IT IS MADE OF NATURAL FIBRES.

LOUNGING 59

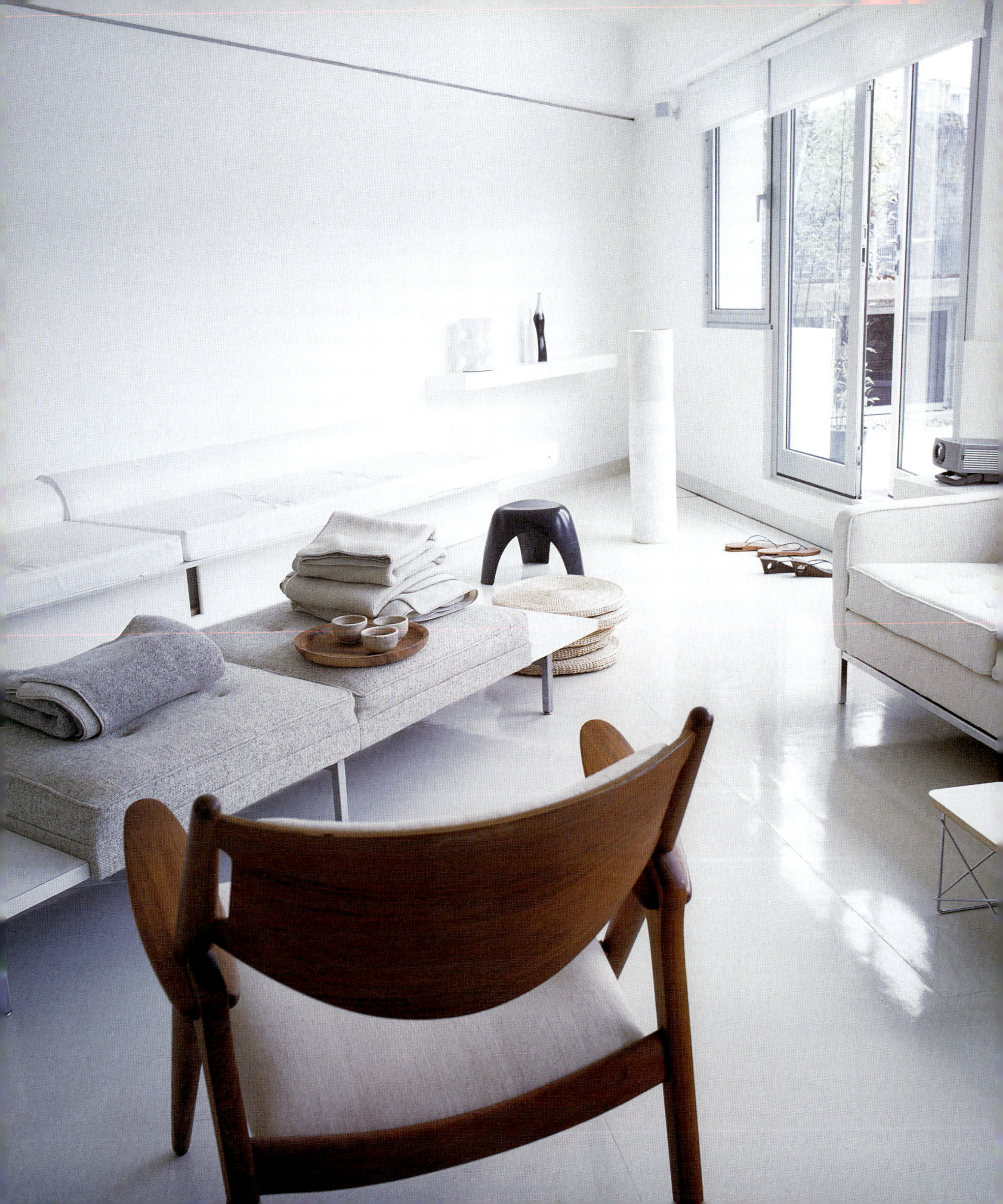

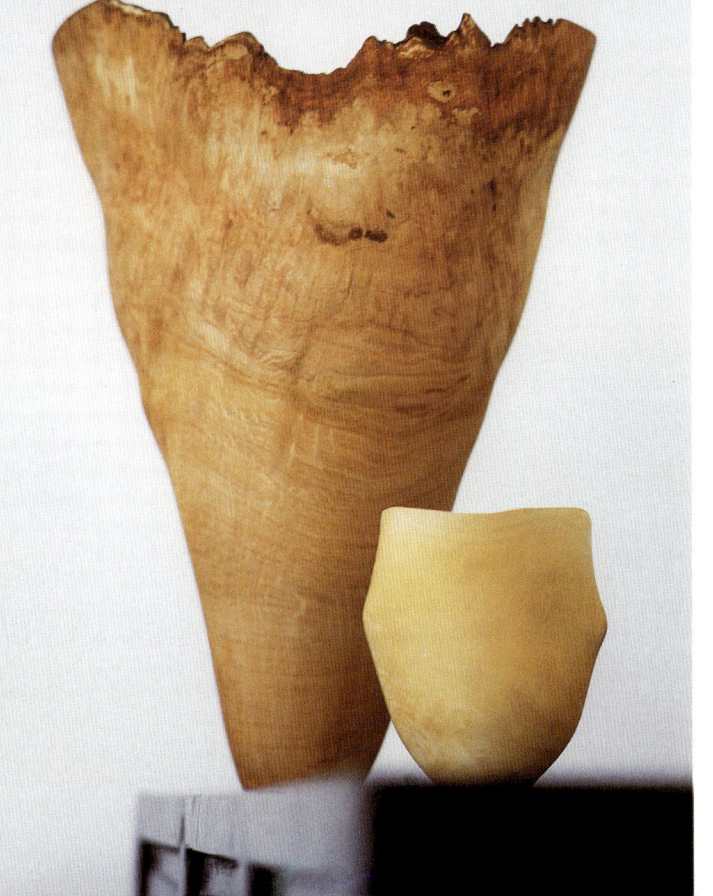

ORGANIC, FLOWING SHAPES, NATURAL TEXTURES AND RECYCLED MATERIALS ARE KEY: BULBOUS CERAMIC VASES, CURVY WOODEN CANDLESTICKS, BASKETS MADE OF DISCARDED PLASTIC, INDUSTRIAL PRODUCTS, RECYCLED PAPER OR PACKAGING.

DON'T OVER-ACCESSORIZE YOUR ECO HOME WITH NATURAL BITS AND PIECES. SIMPLICITY WORKS BEST. FOR A CLEAN AND CONTEMPORARY LOOK, STICK TO PARED-DOWN FURNITURE SUCH AS THIS DAYBED (OPPOSITE), OR ARMCHAIR (ABOVE LEFT), AND CHOOSE JUST ONE OR TWO ORGANIC OBJECTS IN MODERN SHAPES, SUCH AS THIS ROUGH-HEWN WOODEN VASE (LEFT).

LOUNGING 61

ART AND SCULPTURE

How can you be eco-friendly when you're choosing art for your home, you may wonder. You'd be surprised. As well as opting for organic-looking pieces, which are often inspired by nature (a sculpture after Barbara Hepworth, perhaps, a sinuous Secessionist work or a Georgia O'Keeffe painting), you can go even greener by displaying natural objects in an artistic way. Try tall stems of bamboo in a sleek wooden pot – the current trendy choice – sculptural blocks of wood in interesting shapes, heart-shaped leaves arranged in a simple clip frame, or even a row of beach pebbles placed along a mantelpiece.

Alternatively, give a grittier, urban edge to a modern room with a sculpture made from scrap iron or a piece of art that is a testament to recycling. The recycled 'genre' isn't just made up of shock value conceptual art (dirty nappies et al); it can be far more subtle. The Dadaist and Pop artists, who created ironic collages out of recycled rubbish, were brilliant exponents of it. Kurt Schwitters, for example, used random collections of non-art to create art, assembling discarded packaging, old envelopes, newspaper cuttings and bus tickets to form abstract collages. As architect and teacher David Greene commented: 'We now have a profession devoted to something called waste management; I always thought that art was the best profession suited to this task. One person's waste is another person's media – did not Rauschenberg re-circulate other people's waste, (and is not) the collage the highest form of waste management?' What's more, if you haven't got the money for a masterpiece, you could always rifle through your rubbish and make your own.

OPPOSITE: ADD THE FINISHING TOUCHES TO THE DECORATING SCHEME OF AN ECO LIVING ROOM BY INTRODUCING PURE AND SIMPLE SCULPTURES IN FLUID, ORGANIC OR ELEMENTAL SHAPES AND WITH NATURAL PATINA.

LEFT: ALTERNATIVELY, FOR A MORE URBAN FEEL, CHOOSE A PIECE OF GRITTY CREATIVE SALVAGE, SUCH AS THIS ERODED METAL SCULPTURE BY CAROL SINCLAIR. THE BEST ECO ART OF ALL, HOWEVER, IS MADE OF WASTE, SO RUMMAGE IN YOUR RUBBISH FOR ARTISTIC INSPIRATION.

elemental
abstract

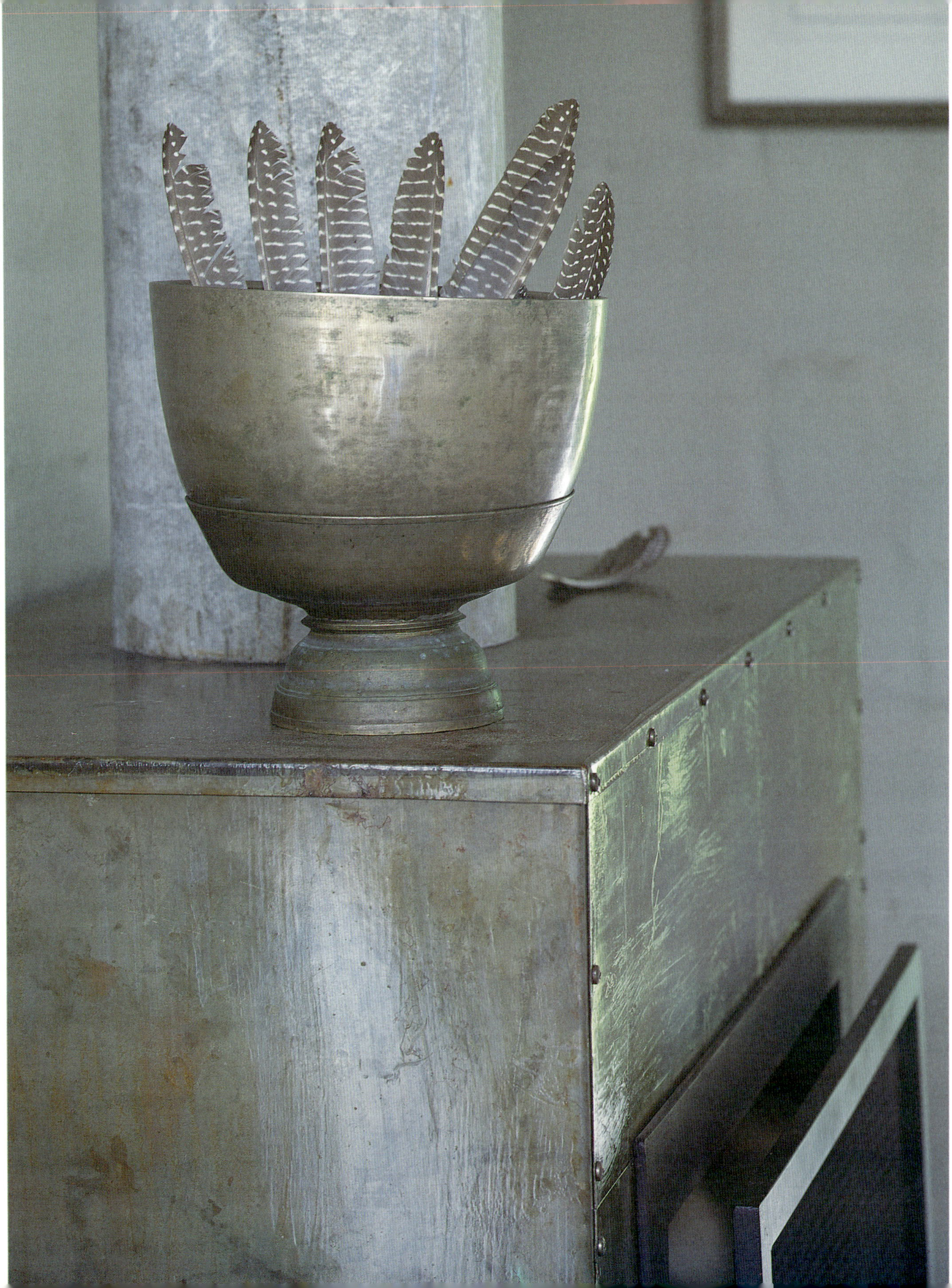

nitty gritty

It's all very well being eco-friendly and organic with regard to the superficial aspects of your home – your choice of decorating materials, cleaning products, food and the like, but what about the other fundamental elements? There are certain aspects of modern life that we simply cannot do without: the comforts of central heating and air conditioning, for example. Moreover, potentially environment-damaging technology, in all its many guises – stereos, televisions, microwaves, mobile phones, computers – inevitably plays an important role in most contemporary homes.

HEATING

Open fires are warm and welcoming, but they are very inefficient as far as the loss of energy is concerned; conventional electrical central heating, meanwhile, uses up vast amounts of energy and is also considerably polluting; a gas-fired system is less harmful to the outdoor environment (its production releases around 40 per cent less carbon dioxide into the atmosphere), but it can pollute indoor air – as can oil or paraffin heaters. The most eco-friendly option for heating your home is a wood-burning stove, the best models of which are supremely energy efficient and emit low levels of harmful combustion gases into the atmosphere.

Heat-storage stoves can be fitted to existing chimneys, but if you can't countenance the thought of completely overhauling your present heating system, try to be eco-friendly with your heating in smaller ways. It goes without saying that the most obvious way of conserving energy is to have your heating on only when you really need it. Another option is to turn your old newspapers into bricks (a gadget that does just this is available from most good green suppliers) and burn them on an open fire (but see above) using eco-friendly firelighters, of course.

ECO ENTERTAINMENT

An eco home doesn't need to be a puritanical place, devoid of twenty-first century gadgetry; televisions, videos and hi-fis can fit in as long as they are used carefully and conscientiously. All electrical appliances generate electromagnetic fields (EMFs) and static and, by upping the proportion of positive ions in the air, they can increase stress levels. As a precautionary measure, use an ionizer to redress the balance (see page 74), limit the time you watch television and don't sit too close to the screen.

More of a problem with audio-visual equipment is the energy it wastes. Many of us leave the television permanently on standby, for example, which can mean that, even when it is not in use, it is still consuming a quarter of the energy it uses when it is turned on. Anna Kruger comments: 'Friends of the Earth have estimated that the wasted energy from TVs that have not been properly switched off costs £12 million per year and generates almost 200,000 additional tonnes of carbon dioxide.' And the answer to this? Stop using the remote control and switch off the television at the wall.

WOOD-BURNING STOVES (LEFT) ARE SUPREMELY ENERGY EFFICIENT AND CAN BE FITTED TO AN EXISTING CHIMNEY. IF YOU WANT TO HANG ON TO YOUR OPEN FIRE, HOWEVER, MAKE IT MORE ECO-FRIENDLY BY BURNING RECYCLED NEWSPAPER AND BY LIGHTING IT WITH FIRELIGHTERS SUCH AS THESE (RIGHT) – MADE FROM SALVAGING THE STUMPS OF PINE TREES IN MANAGED FORESTS.

working

Many of us spend half our working lives in an office, be it outside or inside the home, yet most working spaces are damaging to our health and to the environment. They are full of electrical equipment that eats up energy and VDUs that increase our stress levels, furniture that damages our backs and synthetic materials that pollute the air. Then there is the question of waste. An office generates an endless supply of used paper, old pens, defunct disks, obsolete computer equipment – things that are classified as rubbish and thrown in the bin. If we are employed in a conventional office, there is little we can do other than campaign for change, but at home we can redress the balance. By understanding the impact of our work space on the environment, we can create a home office that is efficient and eco-friendly, hi tech but healthy.

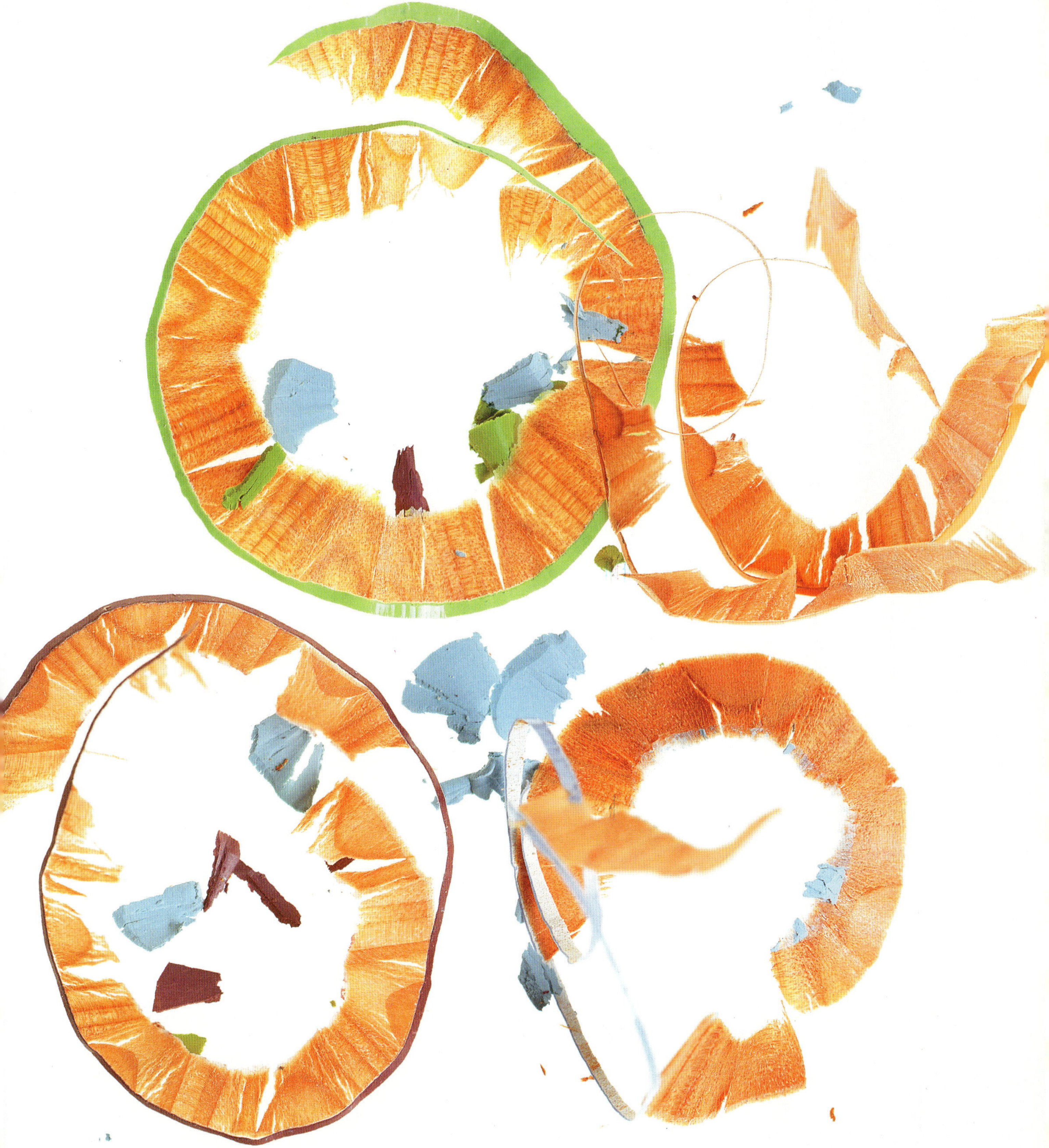

the office

It seems simple common sense to suggest that an office should be bright, airy and comfortable, that it should use bold colours, organic shapes and living accessories – plants, flowers, even fish.

Ergonomic office design has never been high on the list of company priorities. Big corporations have traditionally wanted cost-effective, productive space to house their workforce, but have generally thought little about the impact of the office environment on the individual or the planet. Consequently, office design has very often been thoughtless, unimaginative and sometimes even downright harmful: walls awash with dull-coloured chemical-filled paints, floors covered in synthetic carpet, windows sealed and old air-conditioning systems recirculating stale, polluted air and helping to increase the spread of germs. With realities such as these, is it any wonder that Sick Building Syndrome is now a recognized health problem right across the world?

design

It seems common sense to suggest that an office – the place where we spend a large part of our time – should be bright, airy and comfortable. At home this formula should be far easier to follow, but these days any work space has to accommodate all manner of unconducive elements: the computer that generates radiation, static and heat; the laser printer that gives off ozone; the photocopier that might emit carbon dioxide.

The solution is simply to do what you can to make your office a healthier place. Use natural materials for the walls and floor, choose ergonomic functional furniture, maximize daylight and compensate for all that technical equipment by upping the human factor with bold colours, organic shapes and living accessories – plants, flowers, even fish.

LEFT: THE HOME OFFICE OF ECO FASHION DESIGNER, RAY HARRIS, HAS BEEN ERGONOMICALLY DESIGNED FOR MAXIMUM COMFORT AND EASE.

RIGHT: BRIGHT, AIRY AND DOTTED WITH GREENERY, THIS DUTCH OFFICE HAS ALL THE ELEMENTS OF A HEALTHY WORK SPACE.

ARE YOU SITTING COMFORTABLY?

Choose office furniture that is comfortable and that encourages good posture. Chairs should be height adjustable and give proper support to the small of the back. A foot rest also helps you sit correctly. Desks should be big enough to accommodate all your technical equipment with room to spare so that you don't feel cluttered or hemmed in when you are working. This may sound obvious, but many home-workers make do with chairs and desks that won't fit anywhere else in the house and end up with a bad back or even RSI (repetitive strain injury). If you are not sure what to buy, get advice from office-furniture suppliers or ergonomic specialists and try second-hand dealers (some of the best ergonomic furniture was made 40 or 50 years ago, see page 46). And do all you can, of course, to choose pieces made from natural materials.

BELOW: TAKING THE ART OF RECYCLING TO NEW HEIGHTS, THIS STUDY IS CONTAINED IN A METAL DRUM, WHICH HAS BEEN TACKED ON TO THE END OF A CORRIDOR.

COMPENSATE FOR ALL THAT DULL GREY OFFICE MATTER WITH A MIX OF COLOURFUL FURNITURE AND ACCESSORIES IN NATURAL TEXTURES AND COMFORTABLE ROUNDED SHAPES.

ergonomic

eco techno

Choose equipment that is attractive as well as efficient; invest in approved energy-saving or health-protecting gadgets and keep the most polluting products out of the room.

Computers, printers, scanners, phones, faxes ... the quota of technical equipment that a modern office must house grows by the day. If you are working from home it can be hard to know quite how to deal with it. Designed by technicians, these habitually grey and unaesthetic-looking products might keep you at the cutting-edge of global communication, but will do little to make your office feel or look good.

The arrival of the funky, colourful iMac hopefully heralds a change in the design of office equipment and points the way towards a new kind of working environment where the human element is no longer neglected. For the time being, choose equipment that is attractive as well as efficient; invest in approved energy-saving or health-protecting gadgets (an anti-static screen, for example) and keep the most polluting products (particularly the photocopier) out of the room.

A BRILLIANT COMBINATION OF THE HI TECH AND THE HUMAN, THE COLOURFUL, PERSONABLE, SHAPELY IMAC (LEFT) AND IBOOK (RIGHT) HOPEFULLY HERALDS THE START OF A NEW ERA OF COMPUTER DESIGN.

THE ENERGY ISSUE

All electrical equipment uses up energy, so make sure you switch off any machines when they are not in use and buy products that are as eco-friendly as you can. Some computers have in-built energy savers, which switch off the screen or even the machine itself when it has not been used for a period of time. Look for government-approved low-energy labels (the US Energy Star system, for example) and ask suppliers about wattage levels and energy-saving features. Note, too, that flat screens, such as those used in laptop computers, use less energy than conventional screens and also emit less radiation.

RECYCLE WHAT YOU CAN

We all want to trade in our old computer for the latest model, and as technological advances speed up, this process is happening more and more frequently. Do not be tempted to throw your old monitor in a skip, however. Sell it to a second-hand dealer, auction it on-line or ask your original supplier or the manufacturer for suggestions as to where you might send it. Computer recycling centres, where supposedly obsolete machines are reconditioned for use by schools or charities are on the increase. Look on the Internet for details of facilities near you (the American PEP website, www.microweb.com/pepsite, offers an international directory of computer recycling programmes, for example).

GREENHOUSE ...OR GREENHOUSE EFFECT?

Indoor air quality can be far more polluted than outdoor air these days and nowhere is it worse than in an office. Not only do some pieces of office equipment give off harmful gases, but all electrical devices deplete the level of negative ions (electrically charged molecules) in the air, thereby contributing to feelings of stress and tension. An ionizer, a negative ion generator, will help to redress the balance, and plants can also act as air filters. Aloe vera, bamboo palm, chrysanthemums and spider plants are considered among the most effective natural filters. Before you rush to the nursery, however, consider the following advice from America's 'Queen of Green'., Debra Lynn: 'The scientific tests that prove the effectiveness of plants at removing pollutants were done with one plant in a 12-cubic-foot area. An average 9 × 12 room with an 8-foot ceiling is 864 cubic feet, so you would need 72 plants to duplicate the results – a virtual jungle.'

RECYCLING IS DE RIGUEUR IN THE ECO OFFICE, SO BUY RECYCLED PAPER (LEFT) AND THINK OF WAYS OF REUSING YOUR OWN RUBBISH. EVEN OLD TIN CANS CAN MAKE FUNKY OFFICE STORAGE (RIGHT).

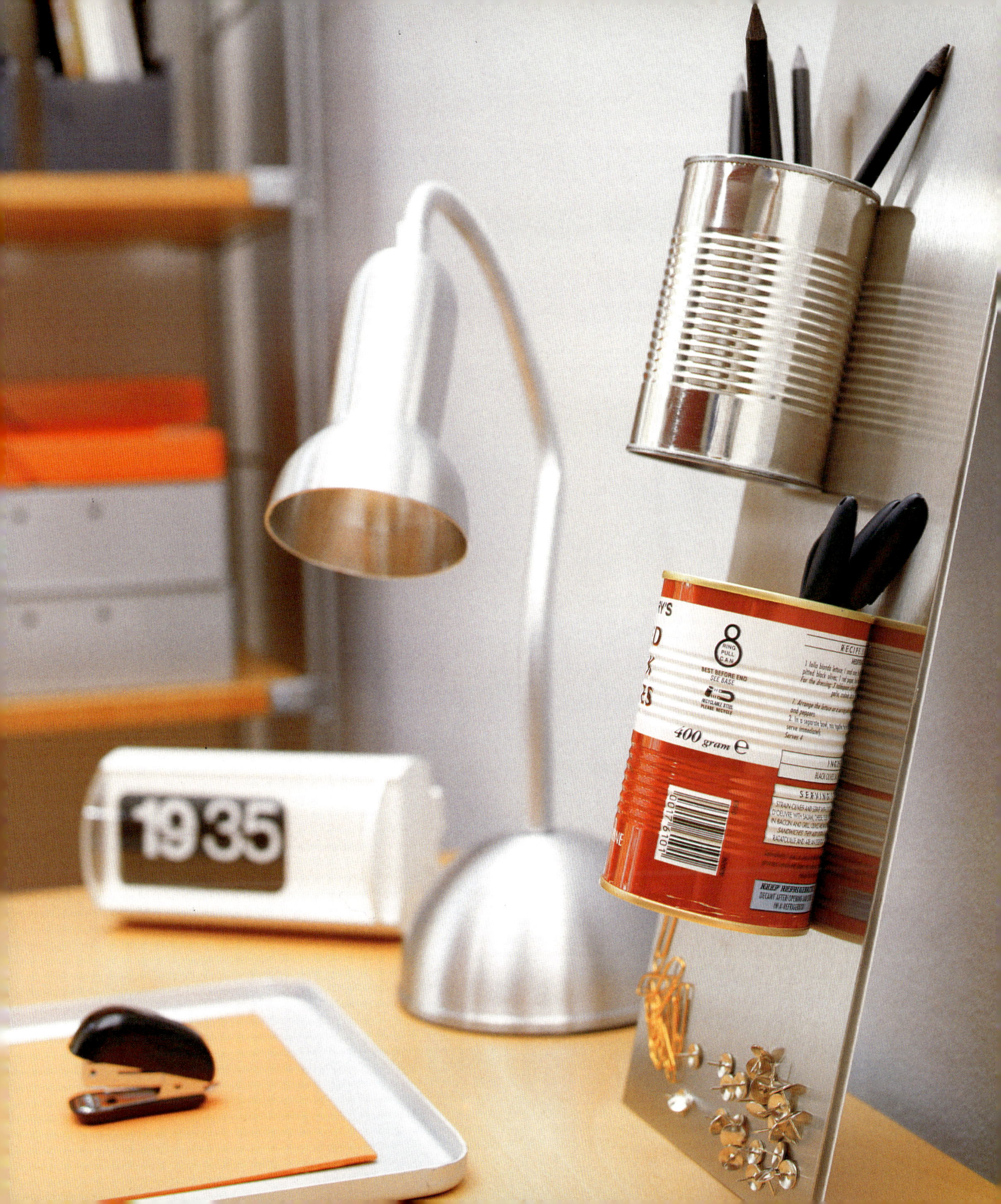
1935
BEST BEFORE END
SEE BASE
400 gram

eco office kit

The first rule of an eco office is to think before you chuck and to recycle as much as you can – used paper should be taken to a waste paper collection point and toner cartridges should be returned to the manufacturer. By ridding your 'rubbish' of the recyclable and reusable, you will find there is a lot less of it to throw in the dustbin.

OFFICE SUPPLIES

Whatever your line of work, it is likely that your office will be full of the usual quota of expendable supplies – paper and pens, disks and diaries, ink cartridges for the printer. These are things that many of us routinely throw away, but shouldn't. The first rule of an eco office is to think before you chuck and to recycle as much as you can. Used paper should be stashed in piles and taken to a waste-paper collection point (see below), and toner cartridges should be returned to the manufacturer who can reuse them (the same can be done with telephones, incidentally). By ridding your 'rubbish' of the recyclable and reusable, you will find there is a lot less of it to throw in the dustbin.

Make sure, too, that you buy as much eco-friendly office equipment as you possibly can, whether it is recycled paper, salvaged furniture, a clockwork radio or green computer accessories. You can even get recycled disks that have been put through a thorough electronic, magnetic, physical and software cleaning system.

RECYCLE YOUR PAPER

The number of trees felled in one year to keep us all in paper and paper products beggars belief – for the UK alone, the estimated figure has been set at more than a million. Increasingly these are rainforest trees, the destruction of which is having devastating consequences (see page 131). Even worse, much of this perfectly recyclable paper, once it has been used, is simply thrown away to join the mass of waste that is engulfing countries worldwide. (Incidentally, paper takes up much more room in a landfill dump than plastic.)

LEFT: ADD A COLOURFUL AND PERSONAL TOUCH TO YOUR DESKTOP BY COVERING NOTEBOOKS, PEN-HOLDERS AND OTHER OFFICE KIT IN UNWANTED SCRAPS OF FABRIC.

RIGHT: FORGET THE DULL DAYS OF COARSE BROWN RECYCLED STATIONERY; THE NEW-LOOK ECO RANGES ARE AS BRIGHT AS THEY ARE BEAUTIFUL.

WORKING

Most paper is recyclable – lightly inked computer paper is particularly suitable – and recycling it makes sense economically as well as environmentally. 'Recycling waste paper to make new paper is clearly economic,' says Anna Kruger in her book *H is for ecoHome*. 'It represents an energy saving of between 30 and 40 per cent on paper made from virgin pulp and produces less than a quarter of the pollution.'

So, there really is no alternative. Recycling paper is de rigueur in the eco office. Create a separate paper bin to make it really easy for yourself, and when it is full arrange for it to be collected (some forward-thinking governments have already accepted their responsibility to set up pick-up schemes) or take your stash to a local collection point. It might seem like an effort but it will be helping to safeguard the future.

In addition, to stimulate the growth of recycling facilities, when you are replenishing your stationery supplies buy as many recycled paper products as you can and reuse those envelopes (reuse labels are available from most green suppliers).

EQUIP YOUR OFFICE WITH PRODUCTS THAT ARE CHIC AND GREEN, SUCH AS OFFBEAT STATIONERY MADE FROM OLD MAPS (TOP LEFT), SLEEK RECYCLED LEATHER DIARIES (LEFT), OR NIFTY CARDBOARD STORAGE BOXES (ABOVE AND RIGHT). ADDING A FEW ECO ELEMENTS TO A HI-TECH OFFICE IS A SIMPLE BUT EFFECTIVE WAY TO MAKE IT HEALTHIER FOR BOTH YOU AND THE PLANET.

78 WORKING

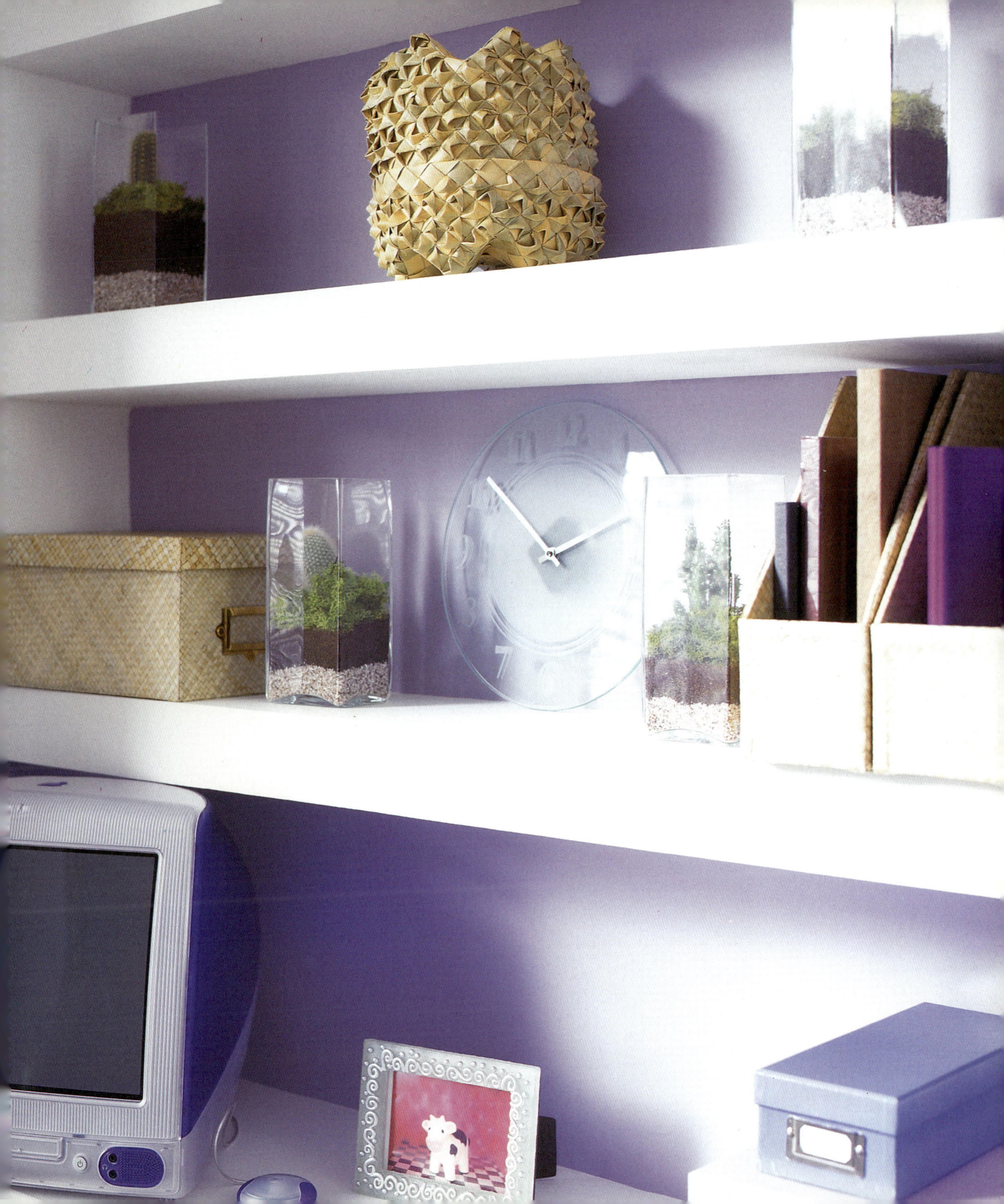

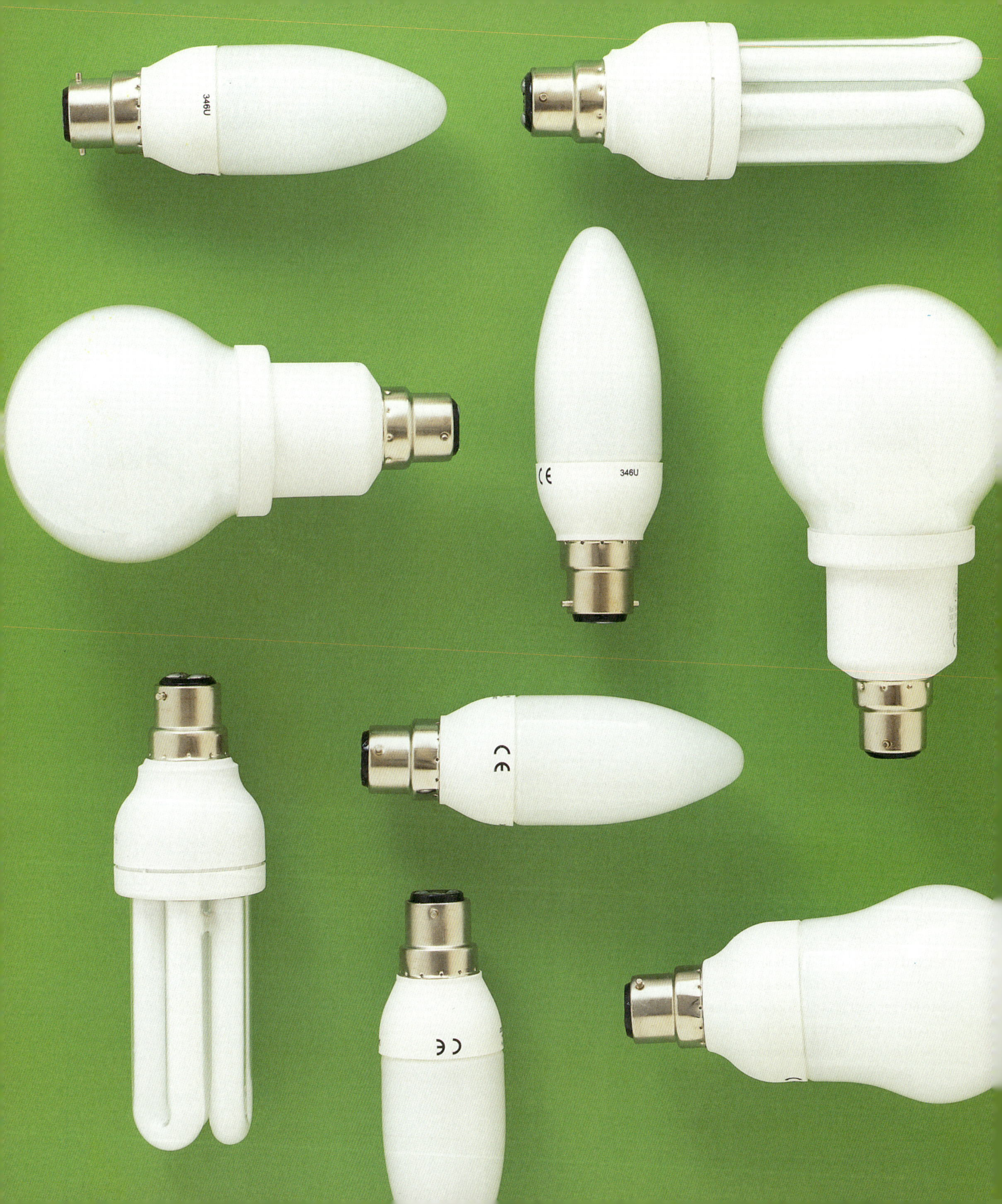
346U
CE
346U
CE
CE

lighting

The most obvious energy consumer is electric lighting – something we have all come to take for granted. As David Pearson notes in *The New Natural House Book*: 'About 25 per cent of the electricity generated in the United States is used for lighting, and approximately half of this amount of energy is wasted, lighting empty rooms or as heat produced by inefficient lamps.' There are simple steps we can all take to reduce the amount of artificial light we use and to keep waste to a minimum.

MAXIMIZE DAYLIGHT

We thrive on daylight and in an office where we want to function as effectively as possible, it is particularly important. If you work from home, place your work space in the area with the most natural light; if the interior of your house is generally gloomy, think of enlarging the windows, installing a skylight or, if all else fails, using light, bright paints to accentuate what little sunlight there is. If you work in a conventional office, persuade the management to switch from incandescent lights (ordinary light bulbs) and old flickering fluorescent tubes (low on energy but not easy to work under) to full-spectrum lamps. These simulate daylight more effectively, although they may also emit higher levels of UV than other lights.

TURN IT OFF

Get into the habit of turning off lights when they are not in use and install modern gadgets – dimmer switches or timers for example – that will also help to reduce waste. Best of all (although it is the most expensive option), install a remote-controlled lighting system with motion sensors, which automatically switches lights on when you enter a room and off when you leave.

SWITCH TO LOW-ENERGY LIGHTS

There are several eco options available these days and any light that is on for more than a few hours a day should be changed over to a low-energy one. For interior use, the most common are the compact fluorescent lamps (CFLs), which use one-quarter of the electricity of a standard incandescent light bulb and last up to 13 times as long, and tungsten-halogens, which are good for task lighting and which can use up to 60 per cent less electricity than their conventional counterparts. Although the initial outlay for these bulbs may be tougher on your purse, they last a long time (some, incredibly, as long as 11 years) and will save you money in the long run. (Note, however, that some low-energy bulbs are not suitable for use with dimmer switches.)

OPPOSITE: LOW-ENERGY BULBS NOW COME IN ALL SHAPES AND SIZES SO IT IS EASY TO SWITCH TO A GREENER VARIETY.

RIGHT: THE LONG-LIFE LOW-CONSUMPTION E LIGHT BY ITALIAN COMPANY ARTEMIDE SPA IS BRILLIANTLY ECO-FRIENDLY, COMBINING SLEEK MODERN DESIGN AND EFFICIENCY WITH SUPERB ENVIRONMENTAL CREDENTIALS.

bathing

A cold shower in a cubicle, a tin bath in front of the fire, a strip wash before bedtime – bathing in the West used to be a very functional business. Today, however, things have changed. Following the example of those who live in the East, we have allowed bathing to become an altogether more pleasurable and indulgent experience. Our bathrooms have changed from functioning purely as utility spaces into havens of sensuality and bathing has become a great deal more sybaritic. Think of steam baths, soft towels, perfumed candles and scented essences. Our medicine cabinets, too, have metamorphosed into treasure troves of essential oils and holistic treatments. It all sounds very eco-friendly, but is our new style of bathing as green as it seems?

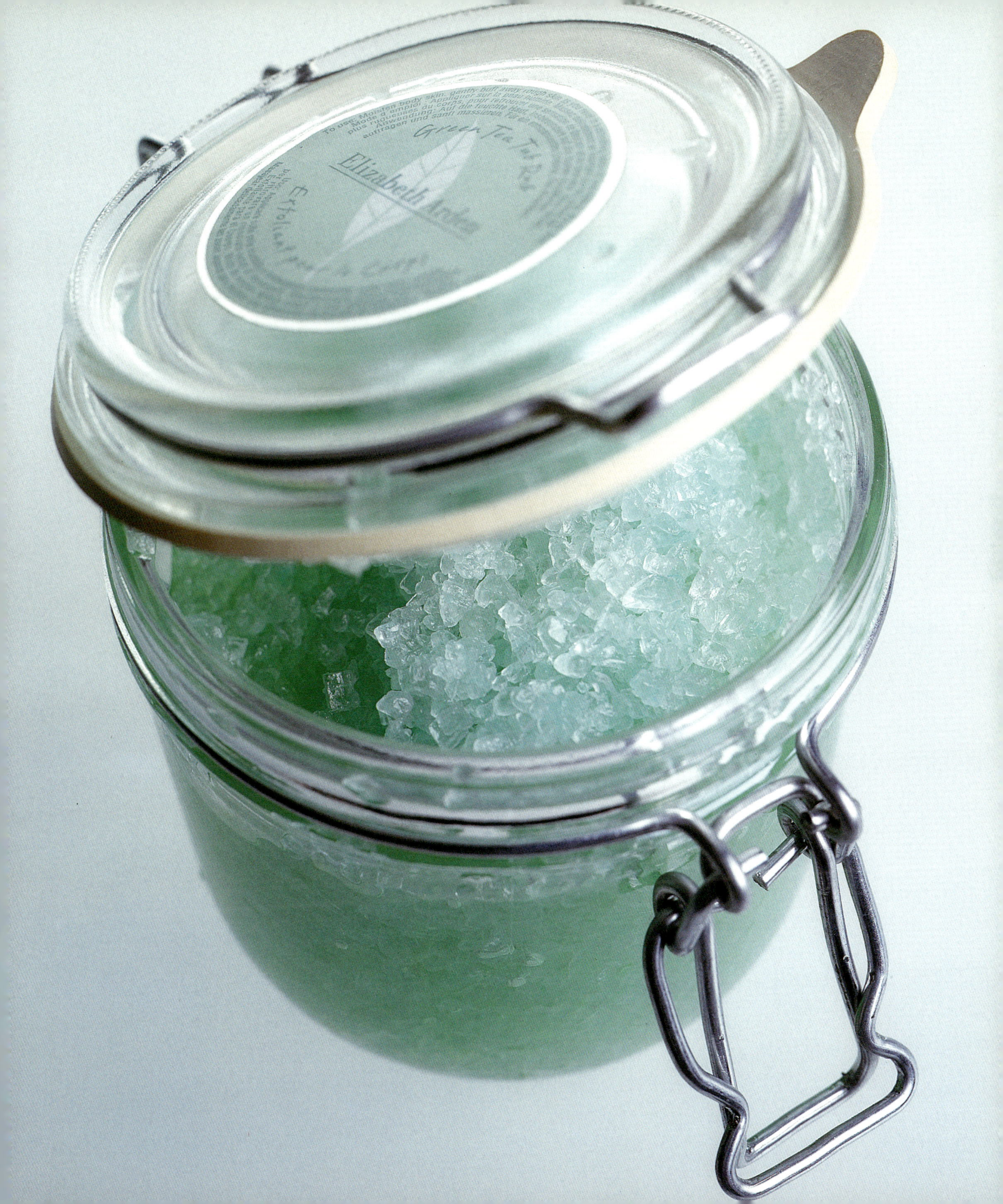
Elizabeth Arden

the bathroom

> Organic materials work brilliantly in a bathroom. Wood, cork and natural paints not only look and feel good, they also allow the room to 'breathe' and thus help to prevent a gradual build-up of mould and damp.

Another prime spot for water and energy wastage in the home, the bathroom is the place where many of our eco-friendly principles can come unstuck. We should be saving water, but cannot do without our power showers; we should be conserving energy, but what about those long, hot baths? There is no ideal solution, of course, but happily some manufacturers are starting to produce mod cons with the environment in mind, so we can appease our consciences to some degree as we bathe.

design

Organic materials work brilliantly in a bathroom. Wood, cork and natural paints not only look and feel good, they also allow the room to 'breathe' and thus help to prevent a gradual build-up of mould and damp – although you do need to ensure you have a good source of ventilation, too. Sleek and chic steel, glass, stone or ceramics are also good for utility areas and will give you cutting-edge good looks and fair eco credentials. The material to avoid is plastic – unless it is recycled – so switch to accessories such as soap dishes and waste-bins in natural woods or canes.

SEXY STREAMLINED SHAPES AND NATURAL TEXTURES ARE ALL THE RAGE IN TODAY'S BATHROOM SO AN ECO LOOK CAN BE THE HEIGHT OF FASHION. CONCRETE – THE MATERIAL OF THE MOMENT – WORKS WELL IN A BATHING SPACE AND WILL GIVE YOU SURFACES WHICH ARE SLEEK, MODERN AND FAIRLY ECO-FRIENDLY (LEFT). AS AN INSULATOR, CONCRETE IS GOOD FOR SOAKING UP THE SUN'S HEAT. IF YOU ARE PLANNING TO WARM YOUR HOUSE WITH SOLAR POWER, CONCRETE WALLS AND FLOORS ARE A GOOD IDEA. SLEEK BATHROOM SEATS, BUILT INTO THE STRUCTURE OF THE BATHROOM MAKE PERFECT SUN SPOTS (RIGHT).

STONE, TILES AND MOSAIC ARE ALL EQUALLY GOOD FOR ECO BATHING AS EACH IS NATURAL, NON-POLLUTING AND EASY TO CLEAN. FORMED INTO SOFT AND CURVY SHAPES, SUCH AS THIS FLUID, CUSTOM-MADE BASIN (OPPOSITE), THESE HARD MATERIALS WILL GIVE YOUR WASHING SPACE ORGANIC LOOKS AS WELL AS LONG-LASTING AND PRACTICAL BATHROOM SURFACES.

THE HARDWARE

Conservation is the key word here, so take steps to reduce 'hardware' consumption as much as you can and, if you are buying new fixtures and fittings, choose the most eco-friendly ones available.

BATHS

Taking a bath uses more than twice the amount of water as a shower, so try not to have one every day or, if you can bear the idea, share your water with someone else – in Japan, the tradition of communal bathing is still very much the done thing. Heating water consumes energy, too, so if you are buying a new bath, it is worthwhile to remember that a small deep tub will hold the heat better than a large shallow one. Similarly, enamel baths are more insulating than plastic or fibreglass versions.

SHOWERS

A shower is the best option for eco bathing and is particularly good if it has a built-in temperature control to save energy. Instead of a PVC-based shower curtain opt for a more natural waterproof screen, such as a bamboo panel or built-in frosted-glass partition.

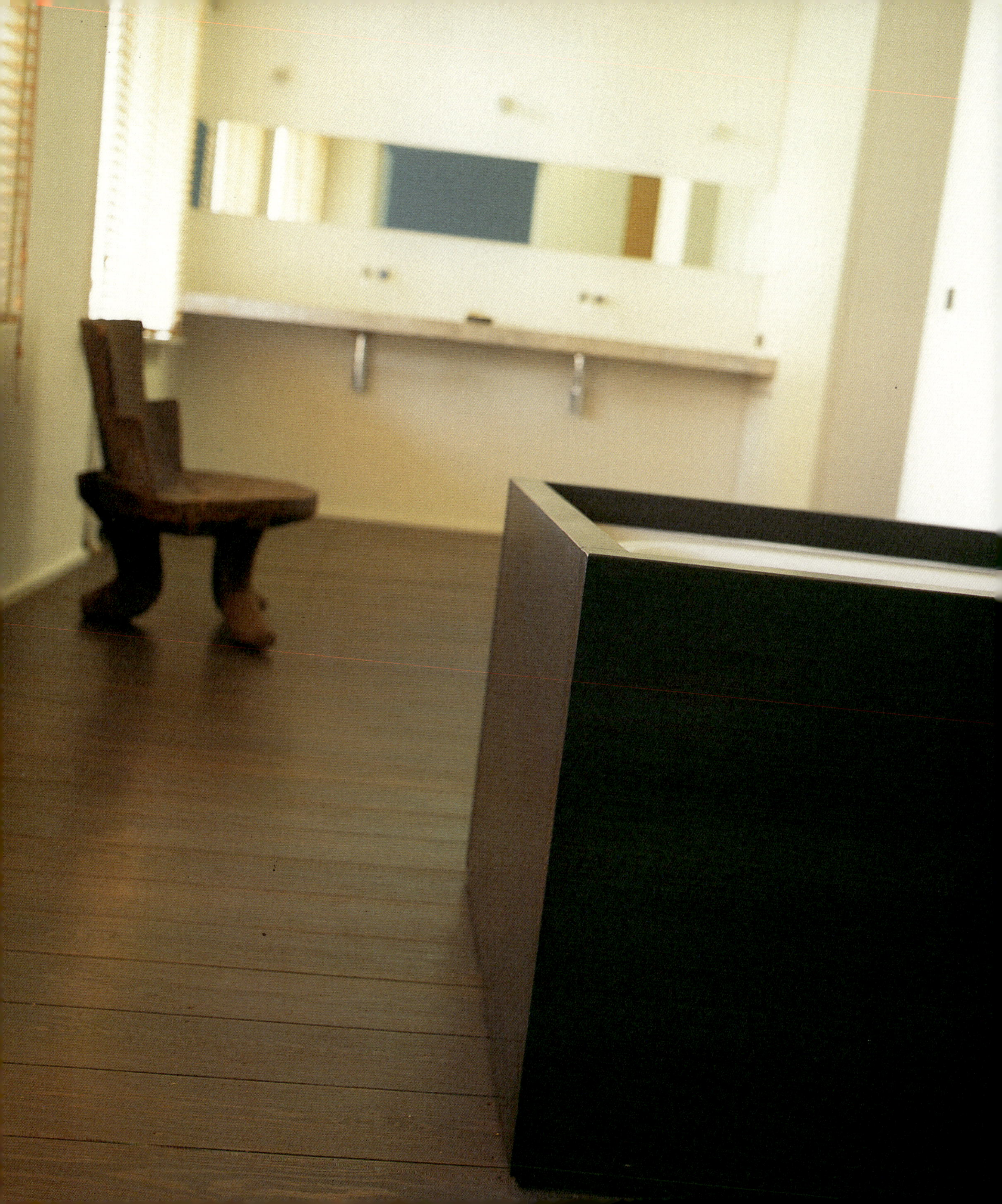

TAPS

If you are buying new taps, invest in those with an aerator, which draws air into the water flow, thereby saving up to 50 per cent of the water, or those with an in-built sensor, which flow only when they sense movement beneath them and therefore cannot be left running. Best of all, of course, are those that combine both.

WCS

These are the greatest water-wasters of all, so if you are buying a new one, choose a dual-flush WC (one with a long and a short flush), which can use as little as 4 litres ($^3/_4$ gallon) per flush – anywhere between 9 and 20 litres (2 and 4$^1/_2$ gallons) is the norm. Alternatively, place bottles of water in the cistern (away from the flushing mechanism) to reduce the volume of water used in each flush. The most eco-friendly option of all is the water-free compost toilet (smell-free, apparently, if properly installed), which saves water and also provides an endless supply of fertilizer! For those of a delicate disposition this may seem a step too far, but eco purists swear by it.

ABOVE: COMBINE SALVAGED WOOD WITH CONCRETE DETAILS FOR A FUNKY URBAN BATHING SPACE.

OPPOSITE: A SIMPLE WOODEN BATHTUB WILL GIVE NATURAL STYLE TO ANY BATHROOM. CHOOSE ONE MADE FROM A HARDWOOD TIMBER FOR DURABILITY BUT MAKE SURE IT COMES FROM A SUSTAINABLE SOURCE FIRST.

THE SOFTWARE

The most obvious eco unfriendlies in the bathroom are the baths, basins and toilets, which waste water and are often scoured clean with chemicals, but your bathroom accessories matter just as much, too. Happily, natural materials are all the rage in this arena as a pared down Eastern aesthetic is the look that everyone is after. Source soap dishes, bath racks and brushes in natural woods (salvaged if possible) rather than tacky plastics and introduce more offbeat textures to add interest – a coconut tooth mug, perhaps, or a bamboo shower screen. An eco aesthetic in the bathroom shouldn't be bare and uncomfortable, but pure and simple, and these natural accessories will give integrity and soul to what is essentially a utility space.

Consider your towels and flannels, too. Ideally, these should be made of organic cotton (or cotton waffle) and coloured with vegetable dyes (or, better still, left undyed) if possible. Most green retailers offer a good selection and you can browse the Internet for on-line suppliers. Don't throw away your old ones in your rush to be green, however; use them to upholster a bathroom stool or to make a tactile cushion.

Finally, the loo paper. Avoid those fat rolls of 'luxury' toilet tissue – if this is the only way you can add luxury to your life, then something is seriously wrong. Instead, switch to recycled paper, which can be just as soft and is far more eco-friendly.

TOP LEFT: GOING GREEN IN THE BATHROOM ISN'T JUST ABOUT SWITCHING TO ECO-FRIENDLY FIXTURES AND FITTINGS; THE ACCESSORIES ARE ALSO IMPORTANT, SO MAKE SURE THAT YOU CHOOSE TOWELS AND FLANNELS THAT ARE MADE OF ORGANIC MATERIALS AND COLOURED WITH VEGETABLE DYE.

LEFT: INCORPORATE NATURAL DETAILS IN UNEXPECTED PLACES TO SURPRISE THE EYE.

OPPOSITE: OPT FOR RECYCLED TOILET PAPER, WHICH YOU CAN BUY IN BULK AND WHICH SHOULD BE JUST AS SOFT AS THE 'LUXURY' VARIETY.

soft

ECO CLEANSING

We are bombarded with 'natural' lotions and potions these days – chunks of seed-covered soap, earthy facial scrubs and grass-green herbal cleansers. But do not be wooed by the packaging – many so-called 'natural' products actually contain man-made chemicals. To make sure you are buying something truly green, read the labels carefully and be discerning. Stick to products that are made purely from plant extracts, that have been produced without cruelty to animals and – if you are an eco purist – that have as many certified organic ingredients as possible.

Organic cleansing does not mean you have to cover your face with avocados and cucumber (although these will nourish the skin), or turn your bath into a witch's brew of herbs and spices (although both sandalwood and lavender, among others, are great for relaxation). Today, green suppliers offer a range of products suitable for the most refined consumer. Personal hygiene is, of course, a very personal business, and finding a natural product that works for you may take a little research and a little more money than you are used to spending. Considering the long-term benefits to both you and the planet, however, it's a price worth paying.

THE CONSUMER MARKET FOR NATURAL BATHING PRODUCTS HAS EXPLODED WITH COUNTLESS COMPANIES CURRENTLY MAKING A PLETHORA OF VITAMIN-RICH CREAMS, SCENTED HERBAL SOAPS AND ORGANIC LOTIONS AND POTIONS. THIS ROSE BUBBLE BATH (ABOVE) IS BY LUSH; THESE HEALTH-PROMOTING, ANTI-AGEING CAPSULES OF GINGKO (RIGHT) FROM ELIZABETH ARDEN.

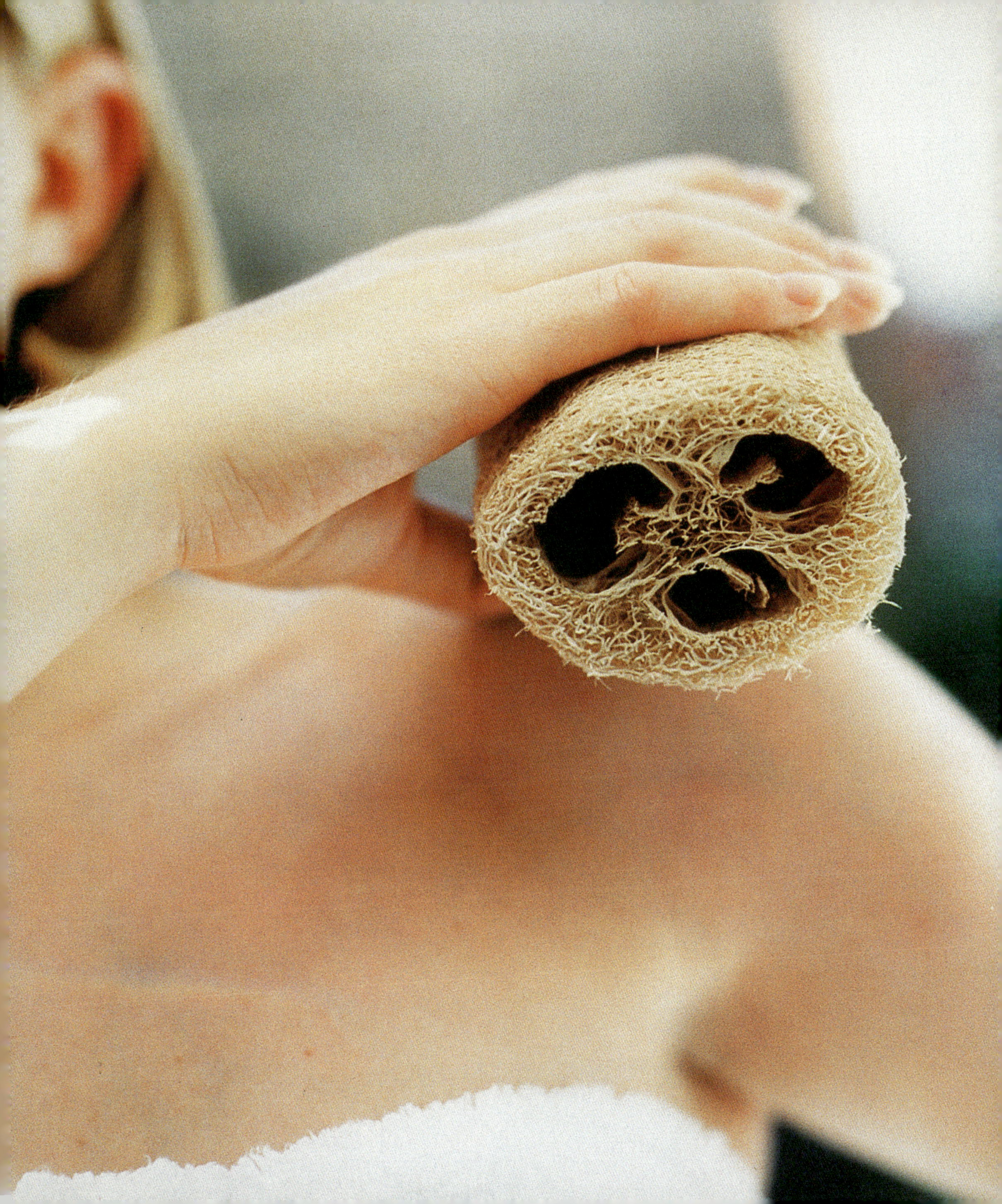

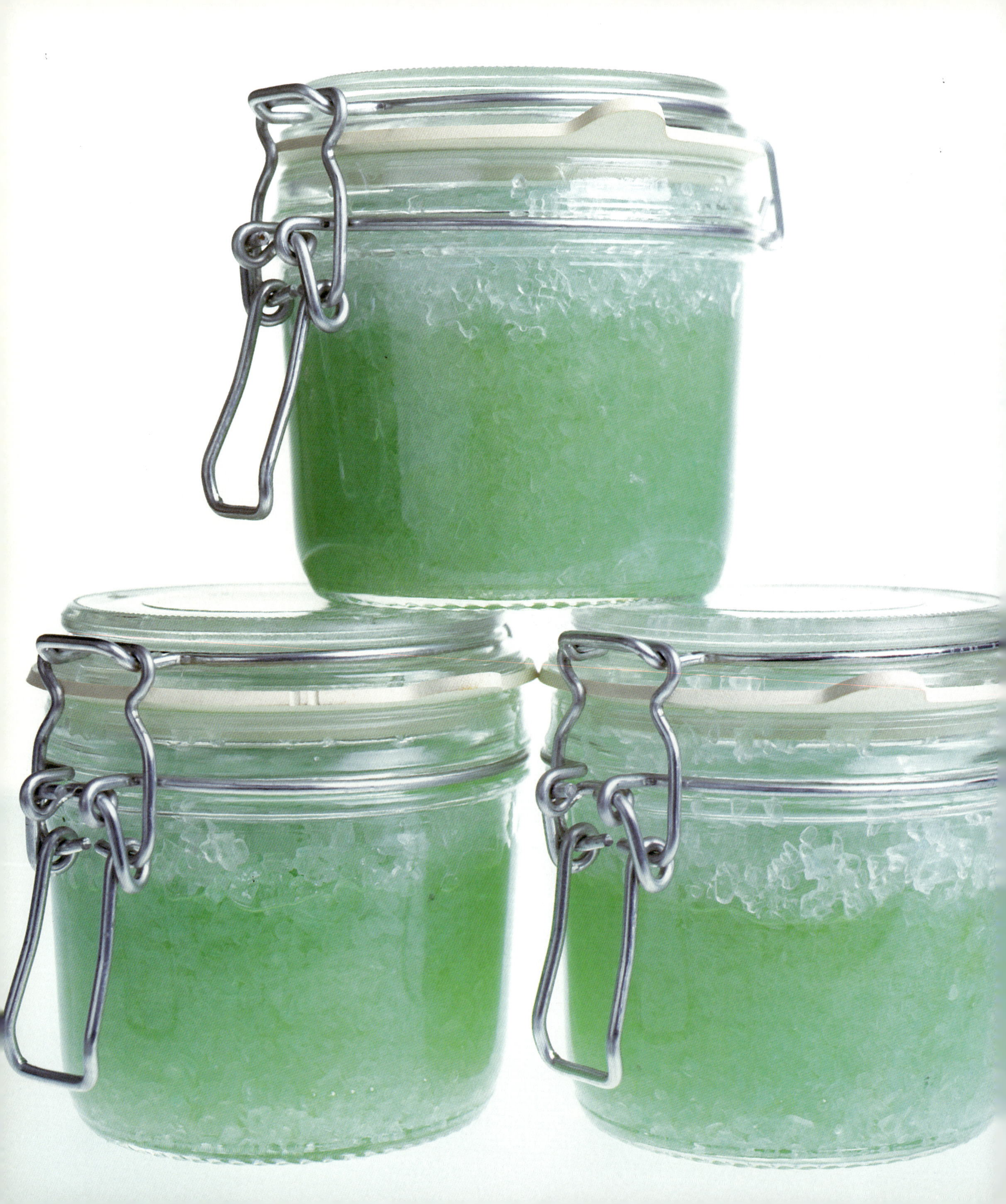

SUSTAINABLE SOAP

Seaweed, coconut, rice bran ... natural soaps come in all 'flavours' these days so choose whichever appeals or go even greener by substituting soap for ground soapnut. This sustainable natural product has been used for centuries in India for everything from body cleansing to polishing jewellery, windows and cars. Its producers claim that it is 'antiseptic, anti-fungal, anti-itching, anti-parasitic, antibacterial, hypo-allergenic and 100 per cent biodegradable'.

HOMEMADE SKINCARE

Save money and cleanse yourself naturally by making up your own skincare treatments, such as these:

- A tablespoon of cornmeal makes a wonderful exfoliant. Use it everywhere, but no more than once a week.
- Use vinegar after a shower or bath, mixed half and half with water, to rid your skin of soap alkalis.
- For a cleansing skin-firmer, spread beaten egg white over your face and lie down until it dries. Rinse with lukewarm water.
- Witch hazel makes a great aftershave and can be scented with essential oil (a few drops per litre).
- Drink lots of water. It's what goes inside your skin rather than outside that makes the difference, and water is the cheapest beauty trick there is.
- Petroleum jelly, mineral or vegetable oil, lard – all these will soften chapped lips and dry hands. Use any one of them at night while you sleep (rub any excess off with a clean cloth).

CLEANSING CRYSTALS

Many conventional deodorants stop you perspiring (which is bad), contain aluminium (which is worse) and, if they are aerosols, may pollute the environment with CFCs (which is worse still). Opt for a natural plant-based, roll-on deodorant instead or make your own by adding a few drops of essential oil to water or vegetable oil. Alternatively, rub more unconventional things under your arms – bicarbonate of soda, deodorant stone salts or even a deodorant crystal, which can last for up to a year.

NICE GREEN TEETH

Common brands of toothpaste may whiten your teeth, but what else do they do? As the brochure for UK green suppliers, Green People, states: 'Almost all toothpaste contains fluoride, preservatives, colouring agents and artificial aromas', none of which are good for you. Many toothpastes also contain saccharin and some include titanium dioxide, both of which have negative implications for personal and environmental health. Opt for herbal varieties instead and remember to turn off the tap while you are brushing your teeth in order to conserve water.

OPPOSITE: GREEN TEA SCRUB BY ELIZABETH ARDEN.

BELOW: HUNKS OF NATURAL SOAP FROM LUSH. IT IS EASY TO GET ECO LOOKS WITH TODAY'S NATURAL SOAPS AND SCRUBS, BUT BEFORE YOU BUY, READ LABELS CAREFULLY TO MAKE SURE THAT 'NATURAL' REALLY DOES MEAN CHEMICAL-FREE.

eco beauty

The only safe, sensible and eco-friendly alternative is to switch to natural make-up, to use cosmetics that are purely plant based and thus good for both your skin and your body.

We all know that beauty is not skin deep, but far fewer of us realize that our make-up isn't either. About 60 per cent of any skincare product is absorbed into the body and, as we discover more and more about what is inside chemically formulated anti-ageing creams and moisturizing lotions, plastering our faces with them seems less and less appealing. The only safe, sensible and eco-friendly alternative is to switch to natural make-up, to use cosmetics that are purely plant based and thus good for both your skin and your body.

BEAUTY PRODUCTS

The skincare industry has become increasingly hi tech and scientific in recent years and any conventional product is sure to contain an array of unnatural ingredients – anything from artificial colours and scents to pesticides – which may do more harm than good to both your skin and your health, not to mention the environment. Natural make-up products, by contrast, are made from flowers, herbs, fruits and vegetables. Far from being dull and earthy, they are far more appealing and romantic than their conventional counterparts – consider foundation made with hand-crushed rose petals or lotions made from nectar gathered from flowers at dawn.

What the natural make-up producers offer is a personal touch (at German-based Dr Hauschka, for example, every leaf, petal and bud is sorted by hand) and their products are gaining a worldwide following. No longer is organic beauty considered the preserve of an eccentric minority, but the stylish option for women everywhere, and celebrities from Gwyneth Paltrow to Joan Collins are happy to put their names to it. While an organic lotion may cost you more than its mass-produced counterpart, when you think of the purity of its ingredients and its manufacture, the price will not seem so great.

WHAT TO BUY

While the range of organic and natural beauty products is growing by the day, distinguishing the pure from the phoney is not straightforward. In Europe, particularly, there is no strict labelling system and although manufacturers are supposed to list all the ingredients clearly on the packet, this information can be misleading. For a product to be called 'natural', for example, it need contain only 1 per cent of natural ingredients. The only solution is to buy big-name 'organic' brands (Aveda, Dr Hauschka, Jurlique, Joy, for example), to get personal recommendations or simply to trust your senses (if something smells chemical, it probably is).

WITH INGREDIENTS LIKE SILK POWDER, CRUSHED ROSE PETALS AND HAND-PICKED HERBS, TODAY'S ORGANIC MAKE-UP HAS LOST ITS EARTHY IMAGE TO BECOME THE SEDUCTIVE, SOPHISTICATED AND SENSIBLE SKINCARE CHOICE OF THE AGE. THESE ORGANIC COSMETICS ARE ALL FROM AVEDA.

GREEN GROOMING

Shampoo, like make-up, has become preoccupied with science. We are bombarded with diagrams and statistics to prove that this or that particular product will give us hair that gleams and shines, and never falls out. What we are not told, however, is that most shampoos contain a wealth of detergents, emulsifiers, thickeners and preservatives, which far from making our hair healthy will do just the opposite (and damage the environment in the process, too). As Green People points out, 'Every time you wash your hair, your skin will absorb some of these chemicals and some will flush into the subsoil water.'

The solution is to opt for the green alternative by buying purely natural products. Eco-friendly suppliers offer a range of plant-based shampoos, hair dyes, tints and conditioners. Alternatively, try creating your own natural hair treatments, which will be far cheaper and can be just as effective.

GO HERBAL

Find out which herbs are good for what, then buy ready-made herbal shampoos or create your own tinctures. Comfrey is good for oily hair, for example; camomile and rosemary help eliminate dandruff; burdock, geranium and lavender are all good for combating dry hair.

USING ESSENTIAL OILS

Add pertinent essential oils to unscented natural shampoos (available from most good green suppliers). Oils such as cedarwood, cypress, lemon, lemongrass and patchouli are all good for combating oily hair. Ylang ylang is good for dry hair.

USING VINEGAR

A vinegar hair rinse discourages dandruff and removes excess oil from your hair. It also cuts through soap and shampoo residues, leaving hair shiny, smooth and soft. Don't worry about your hair smelling afterwards – vinegar's odour quickly dissipates.

CHANGE YOUR DIET

To attain lustrous thick hair, eat garlic, onions, cabbage and nasturtiums, all of which are rich in sulphur, which binds with the protein in hair to make it stronger and more flexible.

NATURAL RUB

One old French country cure for brittle hair is to rub the juice of a raw onion on the roots before you shampoo.

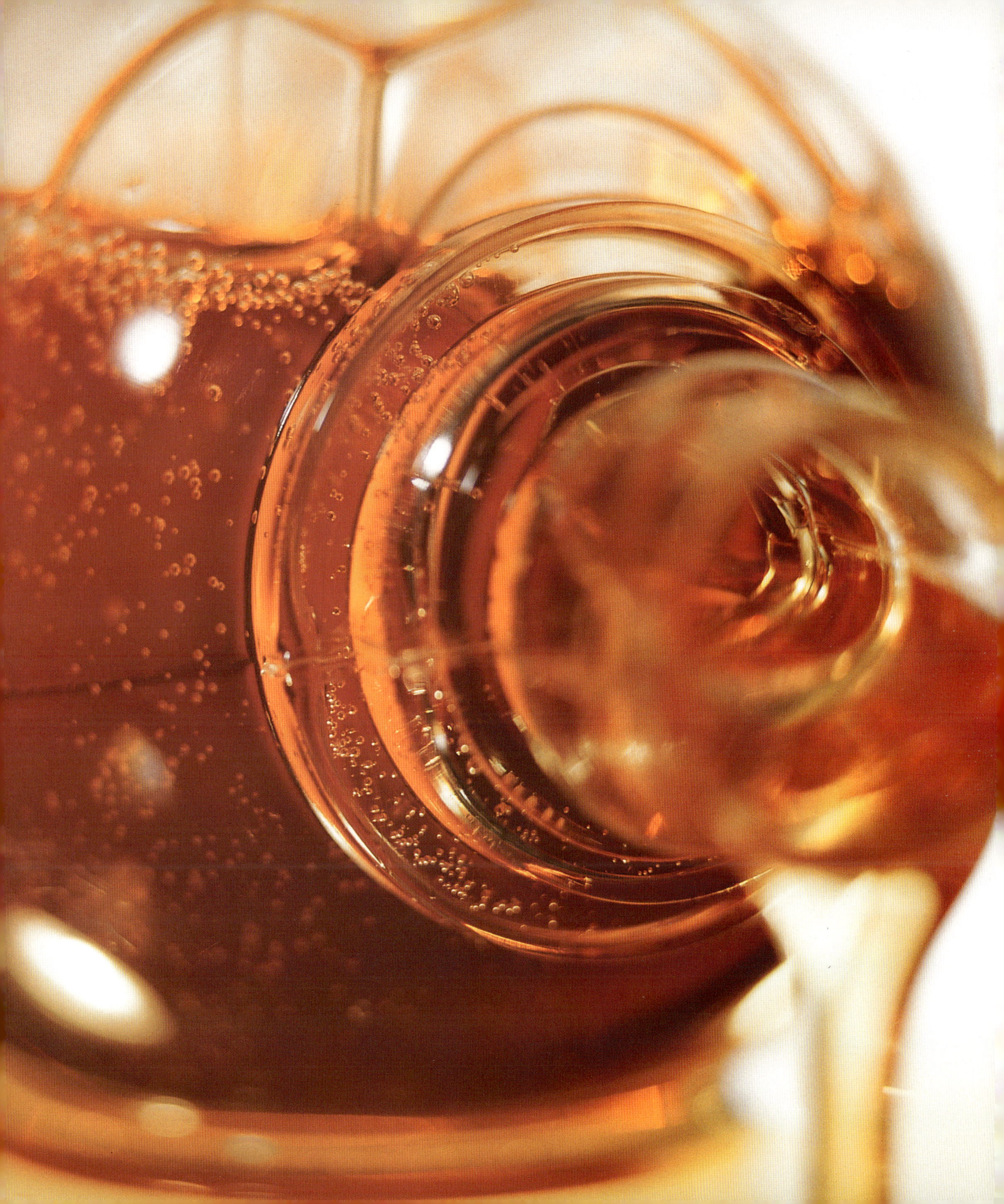

complementary medicine

The term 'complementary medicine' applies to any treatment that is not orthodox. It includes well-known practices like aromatherapy and homeopathy, as well as the more esoteric, such as Reiki or crystal therapy. While each 'alternative' discipline differs in the particulars, they do share an emphasis on holistic healing, which means treating the whole person and not simply the specific symptom.

As natural products take the place of high science in the bathroom cabinet, the same is happening in the consulting room. Over the past 20 years or so, complementary medicine has expanded massively (indeed in the USA it is now the largest growth area in healthcare) and many people who used to dismiss 'alternative' treatments as quackery are now converts to the cause.

The term 'complementary medicine' applies to any treatment that is not orthodox. It includes well-known practices like aromatherapy and homeopathy, as well as the more esoteric, such as Reiki or crystal therapy. While each 'alternative' discipline differs in the particulars, they do share an emphasis on holistic healing, which means treating the whole person and not simply the specific symptom. In today's fast-paced world, where stress, pollution, dirt and noise bombard the body and the mind, this emphasis on emotional as well as physical wellbeing seems particularly relevant.

Alternative therapies also share, in many cases, a long-standing history – some treatments can trace their roots back to the ancient Greeks, if not earlier. In the medical field, it is scientific, pharmaceutical treatment that is the new kid on the block (remember, antibiotics were only discovered after the Second World War).

While it is unwise to dismiss 'modern' medicine out of hand – it very obviously has a vital role to play in contemporary healthcare – so it is foolish to turn our backs on age-old remedies in favour of pill-popping new ones simply because they are new. By using complementary (and often preventive) treatments when we can, we can stay in better control of our health. Working with the natural world rather than against it should mean that we can become less dependent on man-made chemicals to keep us fit.

HOMEOPATHY

Homeopathic remedies come in tablet form and can be derived from plants or minerals. Using tiny traces of substances that mimic the symptoms of illness – thus treating like with like – homeopathy aims to stimulate the body's own immune response. There are over-the-counter remedies available for every health problem imaginable, from rheumatism to travel sickness. Before you try to treat yourself, however, it is advisable to book a consultation with a professional homeopath who will take a detailed medicinal history and who should be better equipped to give you a remedy that will work. It is also worth noting that although the concentration of a particular homeopathic substance may be weak, the impact of a remedy can be dramatic.

NO LONGER CONSIDERED ECCENTRIC, MANY SO-CALLED ALTERNATIVE REMEDIES HAVE BECOME MAINSTREAM TODAY AND SOME HAVE EVEN TAKEN OVER FROM ORTHODOX MEDICINE IN THE TREATMENT OF COMMON COMPLAINTS. HOLISTIC, NON-INVASIVE AND ECO-FRIENDLY, COMPLEMENTARY MEDICINE OFFERS A NATURAL PATH TO HEALTH.

AROMATHERAPY

Using natural essential oils to stimulate or soothe the body and mind, aromatherapy is one of the most popular complementary therapies around. Plant essences can be absorbed into the skin (through massage or baths) or inhaled (by means of an incense burner or vaporizer) to bring you relief from any number of problems. You can even use aromatherapy on your pets. Each individual oil has its own therapeutic properties (see some examples, right) and can provide relief from physical as well as emotional ailments (everything from constipation to catarrh; migraines to wrinkles). In addition, certain blends of specific oils are effective in mood therapy.

When you buy essential oils, make sure you are getting unadulterated oil (you should be able to smell the good ones from the bad) and be prepared to pay for purity. Essential oils are not the same as bath oil, however, so don't use them indiscriminately and do read the attached information carefully to make sure a particular oil will be safe for you to use (some should not be used by children or pregnant women, for example). If you are not sure what effects an oil may have, seek professional advice.

SOME ESSENTIAL OILS

Relaxers: lavender, ylang ylang, camomile, geranium.

Energizers: grapefruit, lemon, clary sage (although combined with alcohol, it can produce nightmares and nausea).

Sensual oils: jasmine, patchouli, rose.

Confidence boosters: bergamot, cedarwood, clary sage, frankincense, jasmine, neroli, rose.

Coughs and colds: cedarwood, cypress, eucalyptus, geranium, juniper, lavender, lemon, peppermint, pine, tea tree – all should provide relief.

Migraine: basil, German camomile, eucalyptus, peppermint, rosemary.

Wrinkles: fennel, frankincense, myrrh, neroli, rose.

ESSENTIAL OILS CAN BE ADDED TO A WARM BATH, COMBINED WITH A CARRIER OIL – SWEET ALMOND OR SUNFLOWER, FOR EXAMPLE – FOR MASSAGE, INFUSED OR BURNT IN AN INCENSE BURNER (RIGHT) TO SCENT THE AIR. WHICHEVER METHOD YOU CHOOSE, AROMATHERAPY OFFERS A NATURAL PATH TO BOTH PHYSICAL AND EMOTIONAL WELLBEING.

uplift

energize

relax

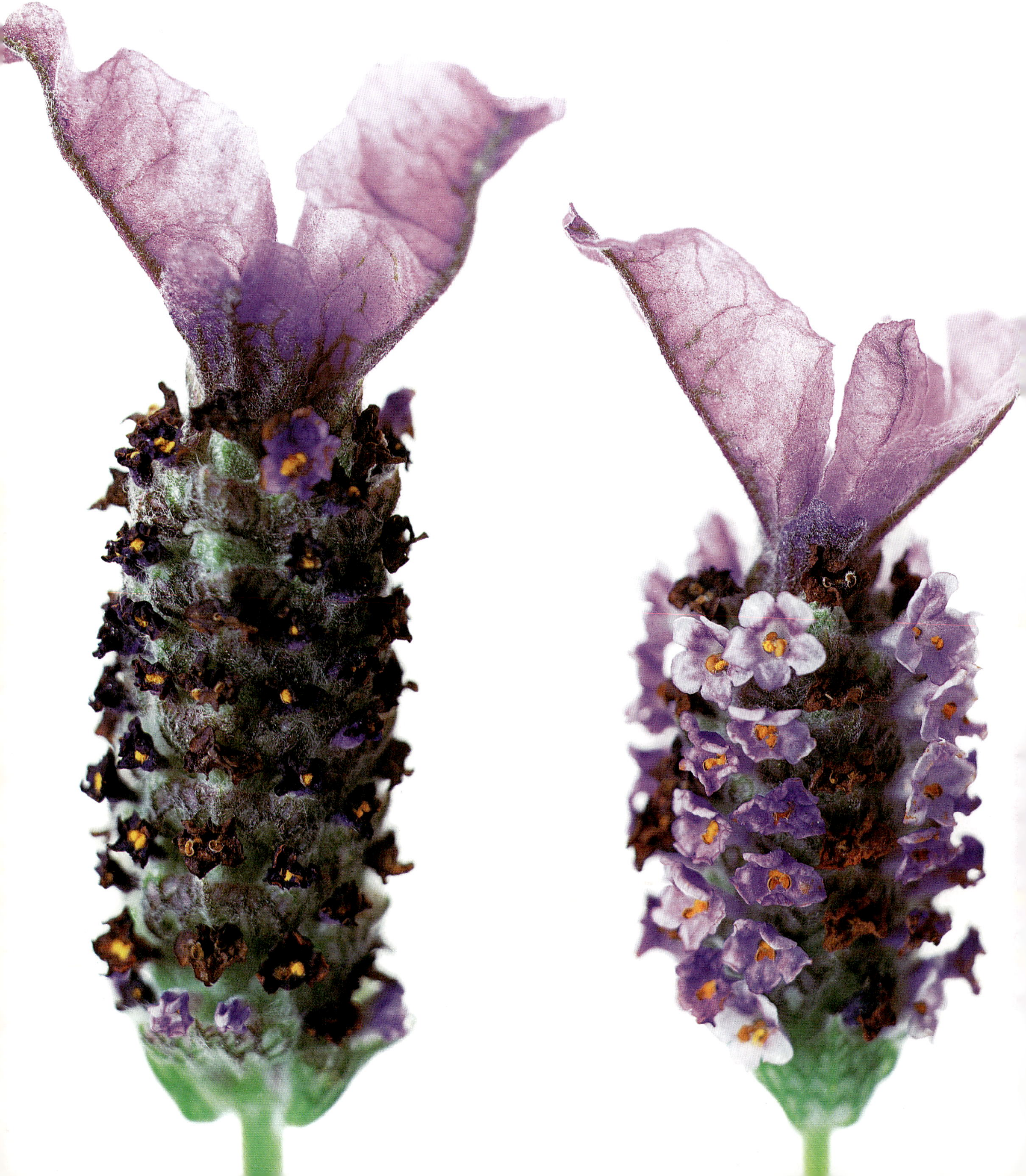

HERBALISM

Curing ills with herbs and flowers is an age-old practice, which is gaining in popularity by the day as we unearth more and more scientific evidence about the very real therapeutic properties of plants. Different herbs have different medicinal qualities and there are many herbal remedies to choose from. They come in various forms – infusions, tinctures, tablets, capsules and creams among others – and suppliers should provide lists of which herbs are best for a specific complaint. See below for some ideas.

Bear in mind, however, that just because herbal remedies are natural this does not mean you can use them indiscriminately. Some can have side effects, especially when taken with certain conventional medicines, so always read the label carefully and seek medical advice if you need to. Also, try to ensure you buy organic products where possible.

OPPOSITE: THE PANACEA OF THE FLOWER WORLD, LAVENDER IS GOOD FOR STRESS AND INSOMNIA. USE A FEW DROPS OF THE ESSENTIAL OIL IN A WARM BATH FOR RELAXATION, OR IN A VAPORIZER TO SCENT THE AIR.

BELOW: ECHINACEA (TOP) IS BRILLIANT FOR CLEARING UP COLDS; GINGER (BOTTOM) IS GOOD FOR RELIEVING SICKNESS.

TO CLEAR UP COLDS
Echinacea: originally used by North American Indians to treat a variety of complaints, this is the biggest-selling natural remedy in the USA. An immune-system booster, it can help fight viral and bacterial infections. **Goldenseal** and **burdock** are also good for boosting the body's natural defences.

TO MAKE YOU HAPPY
St John's wort: also known as hypericum, this is alleged to be the natural answer to Prozac. It supports the nervous system and helps to alleviate mood swings and depression.
Sage: in tea form, sage is known as a woman's tonic and helps to combat depression as well as nervous exhaustion.

TO HELP YOU SLEEP
Valerian: used medicinally for over 2,000 years, it calms the nervous system, helps to overcome tension and aids restful sleep.

TO ALLEVIATE STRESS
Camomile: this is calming but can be mildly sedative.
Valerian: see above.
Siberian ginseng: see below.

TO EASE SICKNESS
Ginger: this aids digestion and helps to relieve both travel and morning sickness.

TO BOOST YOUR ENERGY
Siberian ginseng: properly known as *Eleutherococcus senticosus*, it increases vitality and is good for people under great physical stress (Russian Olympic teams have used it for many years).
Peppermint, **cardamom** and **lemongrass** are also good for boosting energy levels.

TO IMPROVE YOUR MEMORY
Ginkgo extract: often used to treat Alzheimer's, it helps memory and reaction time by improving blood circulation to the brain. It is also a mood enhancer and is alleged to promote longevity.

BATHING 105

FUNCTIONAL FOOD

We rub dock leaves on nettle stings, use cucumber to soothe our eyes and pump ourselves with food-derived vitamins and supplements, but food can offer us much more in the way of medicinal help. Governments worldwide are telling us to increase the levels of nutrient-rich fruit and vegetables in our diets (see page 20), and specifically formulated 'functional foods' are on the increase. For example, some salad dressings have added vitamin E; there are butter-like products that reduce cholesterol, and eggs rich in fatty acids from hens fed with proteinaceous algae. Natural foods can give more medicinal help, too: to treat temperatures, itchy skin and mild burns, for example, a green leaf such as cabbage placed on the spot can do wonders.

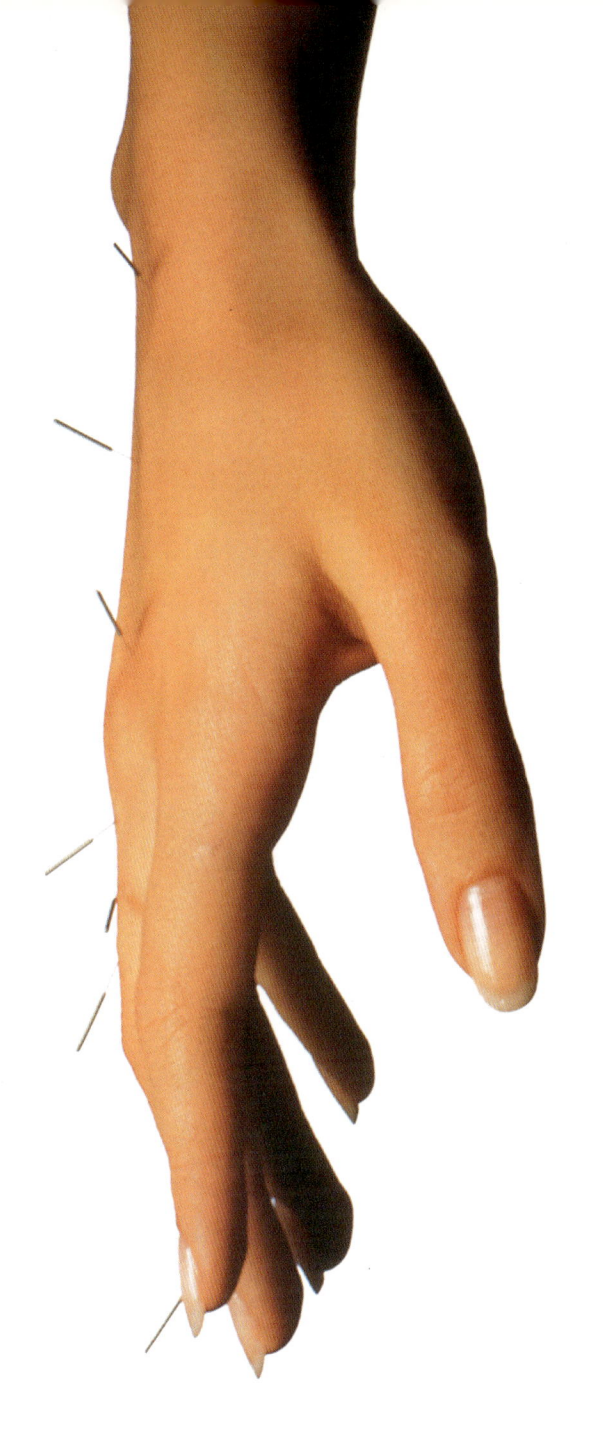

ACUPUNCTURE

It may look like a form of torture, but acupuncture is claimed to be generally painless. One of the best-known therapies of traditional Chinese medicine, the flow of chi (or life force) is encouraged through the body by inserting very fine needles at key sites to stimulate nerve impulses and disperse energy blocks. Acupuncture has a wide following and is said to be particularly effective in the treatment of migraine, asthma, arthritis and back pain.

MASSAGE

Even those who are generally against 'alternative' medicine won't say no to a good massage, whether it is Swedish (the most common and far more innocuous than it sounds), holistic or done only to the feet (as a part of reflexology treatment). By improving circulation, relaxing tense muscles and soothing the nerves, a massage can provide a brilliant non-invasive workout for the body and the mind, and can be even better if performed with aromatherapy essential oils (see page 102).

EVEN MORE 'ALTERNATIVE'

There is a therapy to suit everyone these days – some a little bit more eccentric than others – iridology, for example, analyses the irises of the eyes to detect health problems; Reiki, which cures problems with hands-on healing; and Indian Ayurveda, which offers a complete philosophical and scientific system by which to live. Gaining particular popularity at the moment, however, is crystal therapy. Exponents of the art claim that the use of crystals on or around the body can help redress energy imbalances and boost energy, and even the medical establishment is beginning to sit up and take notice. Catherine Price, a practising British dentist, for example, uses rose quartz crystals to relax anxious patients: 'I'm not a crystal healer, but rose quartz seems to have such a calming effect.'

ABOVE: ACUPUNCTURE IS EFFECTIVE IN TREATING MIGRAINE, ASTHMA, ARTHRITIS AND BACK PAIN.

OPPOSITE: KNOWN FOR THEIR HEALTH-GIVING PROPERTIES, MANY HERBS ARE BENEFICIAL TO THE BODY AND MIND. ROSEMARY, FOR EXAMPLE, HELPS TO STIMULATE DIGESTION AND CIRCULATION, AND ALSO IMPROVES CONCENTRATION.

BATHING

sleeping & dressing

To make sure we sleep soundly at night, we don't just need a healthy environment but a clear conscience, too, so thinking green in the bedroom is particularly important. To create an eco sleeping space, don't feel you need to compromise on comfort, colour or style. Indeed, the latest looks in bedroom décor are big on natural textures, and there are lots of pure materials – wood, organic cotton and raw silk, for example – that can come in very modern shapes and colours, making it easy to be design- and eco-conscious at the same time. As for the clothes and shoes you wear, eco-friendly fashion has truly come of age, so look out for chic outfits made from organic or recycled materials. In the eco bedroom, you can sleep easy in the knowledge that you are doing your bit for the planet.

LILAC

the bedroom

For the bedroom, choose materials that will give you instant cutting-edge kudos – bamboo or cork, for example, untreated grainy wood or funky felt – and add a touch of luxury in the details, be it a soft and shaggy sheepskin rug or some extravagant slinky silk sheets.

design

Natural textures are all the rage in the design world at the moment and the time is ripe for an eco look in the bedroom. Try and choose materials that will give you instant cutting-edge kudos – bamboo or cork, for example, untreated grainy wood or funky felt – and add a touch of luxury in the details, be it a soft and shaggy sheepskin rug or some extravagant slinky silk sheets.

Alternatively, you can go down the recycled route. Use industrial salvage to give your bedroom an urban edge, or introduce second-hand furniture and vintage fabrics for a softer retro style. And remember, don't forget the pot plants – once again, these 1970s staples are becoming hip on the home front.

beds

There are so many designs available nowadays, it is fairly easy to find a bed that is both stylish and eco-friendly. Choose natural materials if at all possible – softwood sculpted into a modern shape, rattan woven into a sinuous organic form (but make sure it comes from a sustainable source) or a sleek wooden base topped with a headboard upholstered in natural fabric.

According to eco experts (as well as exponents of feng shui), metal beds should be avoided if possible because the metal can become magnetized, which could, in turn, cause health problems. If you have a metal bed already, fit a neutralizing undersheet just to be on the safe side or, alternatively, install a demand switch that can isolate a particular electric circuit and cut off the current when it is no longer needed.

If you cannot find a bed base that you like, take inspiration from the East and use a natural fibre-filled futon instead. Alternatively, simply place a natural mattress on the floor for fashionable – and eco-friendly – low-level sleeping.

LEFT: KEEP YOUR BEDROOM PURE AND SIMPLE WITH CLEAN LINES, ORGANIC PAINTS AND NATURAL TEXTURES.

RIGHT: FURNITURE IN CURVY SPACE-AGE SHAPES WILL BRING YOUR BEDROOM BANG UP TO DATE.

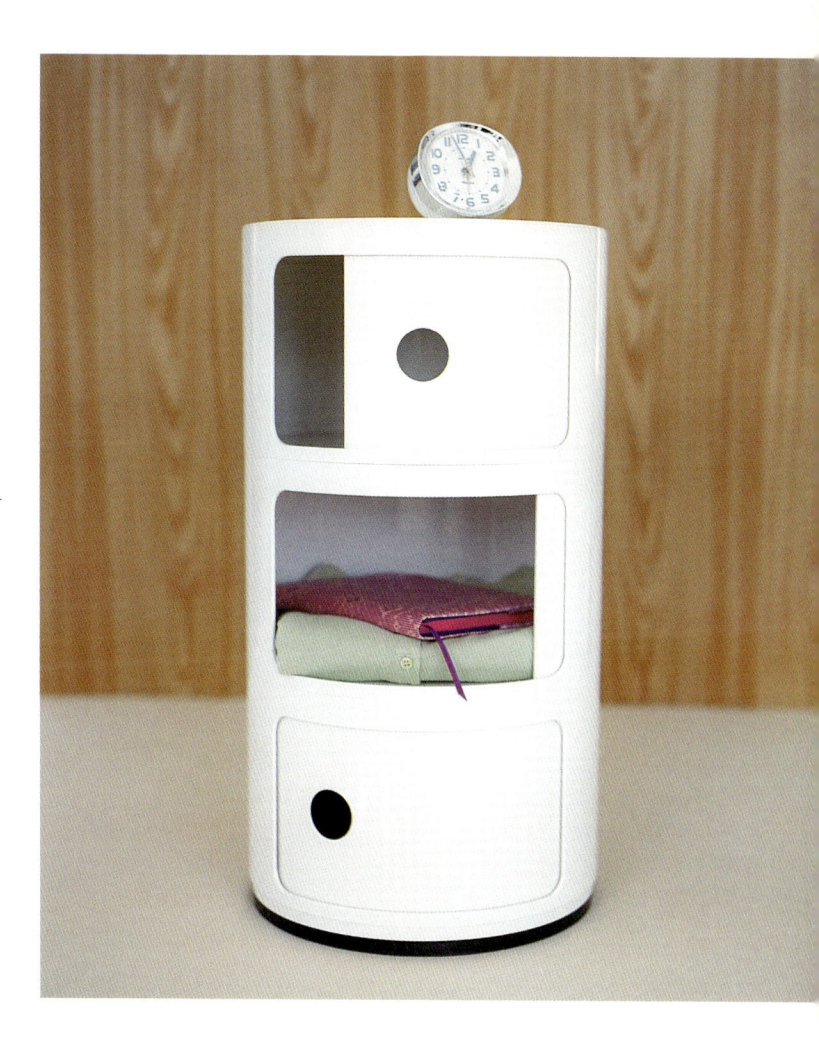

SLEEPING & DRESSING 111

MATTRESSES

We think about how hard or soft a mattress is before we buy it, but few of us consider its eco credentials. We should do, however, since a mattress made of natural materials has no nasty chemicals and is better both for the environment and for us. What's more, natural fibres such as wool, organic cotton or non-allergenic latex soak up sweat far more effectively than the synthetics – a big bonus considering we exude around a litre of it as we sleep – so they should make a mattress more comfortable and longer-lasting.

Most of us know the drawbacks of a very soft mattress, but don't be tempted to opt for an iron-hard one instead as, contrary to popular opinion, they aren't good for your back. Choose an ergonomic mattress that will support your spine, allowing it to curve naturally as you sleep. Waterbeds are very good in this respect and can be the perfect option for allergy sufferers, since dust mites – the cause of the problem – can't survive in water.

DUVETS AND PILLOWS

Soft, warm and light, down-filled duvets and pillows are hard to beat. If you are allergic to feathers, however, organic cotton or unbleached kapok fillings make good alternatives; if you cannot find these, use an organic barrier cover. Steer clear of synthetic pillows in particular, which do not absorb moisture so well and may offgas harmful chemicals. For the ultimate green headrest, opt for a herb-filled aromatherapy pillow, which, so the manufacturers claim, will guarantee you sweet dreams.

LEFT, TOP AND BOTTOM: FOR A FUNKY MODERN TAKE ON ECO, GO FOR EASTERN STYLE – EITHER EXOTIC AND ECLECTIC, WITH PAPER LANTERNS, EASTERN PARAPHERNALIA AND BEDDING IN RICHLY LUXURIANT VEGETABLE-DYE SHADES, OR ZEN-LIKE AND MINIMAL, WITH NATURAL FABRICS AND FLOORING, GEOMETRIC LINES AND A LOW-LEVEL BED.

Paint effect in left-hand picture by Benetton. See page 40 for more information.

NATURAL TEXTURES ARE ALL THE RAGE IN THE DESIGN WORLD AT THE MOMENT AND THE TIME IS RIPE FOR AN ECO LOOK IN THE BEDROOM.

BELOW: TO CREATE A HEALTHY AND CALM BEDROOM, WHERE YOU CAN RELAX AND UNWIND, MAXIMIZE THE AMOUNT OF SUNLIGHT COMING INTO THE ROOM BY CHOOSING DIAPHANOUS CURTAINS OR BLINDS, AND MAKE SURE YOU HAVE GOOD STORAGE SO YOU CAN KEEP SURFACES SIMPLE, CLEAN AND UNCLUTTERED.

ECO SHEETS DON'T NEED TO BE COARSE, COLOURLESS OR UNCOMFORTABLE. OPT FOR CRISP ORGANIC COTTON (OPPOSITE) OR INDULGE YOURSELF WITH PURE SILK (LEFT). WHILE THE MATERIAL IS ENVIRONMENTALLY FRIENDLY, THE DYEING PROCESS OFTEN IS NOT, SO STICK TO VEGETABLE-DERIVED COLOURS IF AT ALL POSSIBLE.

crisp

pure

natural

SHEETS
Considering that we spend almost one-third of our lives lying on them, it is surprising how little attention most of us pay to our sheets. We choose the colour and the size with care, but frequently choose the cheapest material. Much of the bedlinen these days is made of polycotton – a mix of polyester and cotton, which is often treated with formaldehyde to stop it creasing. Try to avoid bedding labelled 'easy-care' or 'non-iron', and if you do opt for a polyester-based fabric, wash your sheets well before you first use them.

The naturals – linen, cotton or cotton flannel – may seem as eco-friendly as you can get, but most shop-bought 'natural' fabrics will have come into contact with various insalubrious chemicals used for bleaching, dyeing and fireproofing. The only true eco option is to buy specifically organic and untreated fabrics, which can be expensive. If you do decide to stretch your budget, why not splash out on silk instead? This luxury alternative is sustainable and, as long as it has not been pumped full of chemical dyes, silk is reasonably green.

BLANKETS AND QUILTS

When it comes to blankets, needless to say, pure wool is what you want. It will keep you warm in the winter months and yet cool in the summer; it is naturally flameproof and also very absorbent (a sheepskin fleece makes a brilliant underblanket for a baby's cot). What's more, a woollen throw will bring a bit of natural texture – the latest must-have – to your bedroom. The only downside is that most wool is chemically mothproofed before it is sold, so try to buy untreated wool if you can.

PATCHWORK

'Make do and mend' is the perfect eco-friendly philosophy, and patchwork is the ultimate thrift craft – a fantastic way of recycling 'waste'. If the idea of quilting is anathema to you, start small. Make a cushion cover first and work up to something larger. Patchwork quilts need not be twee – designs can be funky, bold and graphic. The vintage look is very 'in' at the moment and it is easy to update the concept by incorporating the odd bit of fashion fabric into the mix (that ripped designer dress, perhaps), including a swatch or two of unexpected texture (denim or leather, for example) and adding a trendy trimming.

RUGS

An eco-friendly rug is just what you need to soften a natural wooden floor in the bedroom. Opt for pure woollen ones, coloured with seductively muted vegetable dyes or – for cutting-edge textural looks – an undyed and untreated sheepksin or cowhide (see page 58). Alternatively, top your floor with natural matting – a sisal, coir or jute rug, for example – or, most eco-friendly of all – make your own rag rug, the ultimate in recycled furnishing.

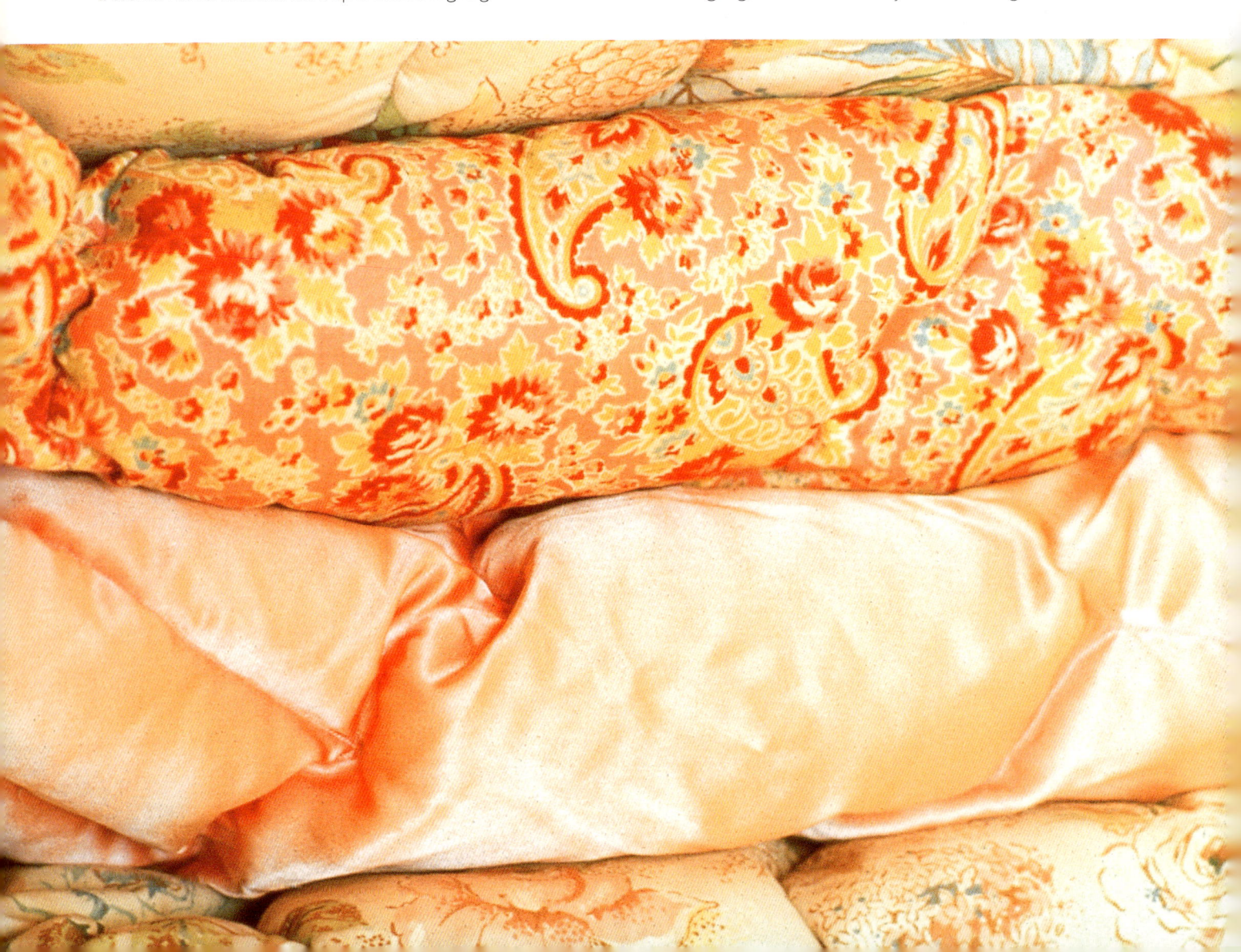

THE VINTAGE LOOK IS HIP AT THE MOMENT AND OLD-FASHIONED QUILTS AND EIDERDOWNS ARE STORMING BACK INTO STYLISH BEDROOMS (ABOVE). FOLLOW THE TREND AND GET YOURSELF ECO CREDENTIALS TO BOOT BY BUYING ANTIQUE OR SECOND-HAND QUILTS, OR MAKING YOUR OWN WITH REMNANTS OF FUNKY FABRIC.

eco dressing

With designers starting to take environmental issues on board, an eco-friendly wardrobe need no longer be filled with hessian smocks and hemp shoes – although even these can be funky in the right hands.

DRESSING IN ECO-FRIENDLY CLOTHES DOESN'T MEAN YOU HAVE TO COMPROMISE ON STYLE. MUCH OF FUNKY FASHION USES RECYCLED MATERIALS AND EVEN HEMP AND HESSIAN CAN BE TURNED INTO DESIGNER OUTFITS. IF YOU WANT THE LOOK WITHOUT THE LIFESTYLE, BUY WITTY NATURAL PRINTS SUCH AS THIS GRASS GREEN BIKINI BY HOLLAND & HOLLAND.

However sound our eco principles over food and furnishings may be, when it comes to fashion, they tend to go by the wayside. We don't usually consider the environment when we rush out to buy those designer trainers or when we dress ourselves from head to toe in funky synthetic fibres. Clothes are the things that define us, and most of us are simply not prepared to sacrifice style in order to be green.

The good news is, we don't have to. While the range of specifically eco-friendly clothing on offer is limited – and much of it, it must be said, still true to the dungaree-and-brown-sandal stereotype – there are ways of dressing green and staying at the cutting-edge of fashion. Some of the latest designs on the catwalk will give you natural looks in an instant (think of Prada's recent leaf-printed fabrics and Camper sandals emblazoned with wild flowers), while others also have good eco credentials. Patchwork dresses and denim skirts made from jeans, for example, are turning recycling into a fashion statement.

Designers, too, are starting to take environmental issues on board. In a high-profile move, Katharine Hamnett famously stopped using PVC in her fashion collections after consultations with Greenpeace, and American giant Esprit is known for the eco bias of its manufacturing. This trend is sure to expand among environmentally aware fashion designers, and an eco-friendly wardrobe need no longer be filled with hessian smocks and hemp shoes – although even these can be funky in the right hands. In addition, advances in technology have led to the arrival of a new breed of recycled and hi-tech fabrics (Polarfleece is just one example), which look set to revolutionize the eco credentials of the fashion industry.

clothing

Natural fabrics are the bees knees for eco clothes, but beware because some of these are not quite what they seem. Cotton and linen, for example – those classic staples of the summer wardrobe – are often treated with chemicals during production (see page 115), while wool and raw silk may be coloured with petrochemical-based dyes. To be truly green, try to find 'organic' clothes (the Internet is a good place to browse), and experiment with more obviously eco-friendly fibres,

SLEEPING & DRESSING

such as hessian and hemp. These natural and sustainable products may sound coarse and earthy, but are today being made up into some stylish and surprisingly sophisticated clothes. An elegant and modern hemp and silk wedding dress (designed by Hess Naturtextilien GmbH) even made it to the shortlist of the UK's 1999 Design Sense award for sustainable design. If you cannot find the look you want in organic clothing catalogues, you could always buy the fabric instead and have it made up into a style of your choice.

FUR, SKIN AND LEATHER
Animal hide might have been man's first clothing but that does not mean that we passive consumers are morally justified in tripping down to the shops for a fur coat and a crocodile-skin handbag. Indeed, we would probably get into trouble with animal-rights campaigners if we did. Calvin Klein was vilified recently for using snakeskin in his collection, and a leading London tailor was forced to back down from plans to make a jacket out of hamsters. Puritan 'eco-chicsters' would probably avoid animal hide altogether, but – arguably – if you steer clear of pelts from endangered species and buy only those that have been produced without cruelty to animals and without the use of harmful chemicals, you can consider yourself in eco-friendly territory. If you do not want to court controversy, however, stick to the fakes – but make sure that they are made of natural fibres.

UTILITY FABRICS (LEFT AND BELOW) ARE MADE TO LAST AND ARE EASY TO ADAPT TO THE LATEST FASHIONS. RUN UP A DENIM SKIRT FROM A PAIR OF OLD JEANS OR ADD A TRENDY TRIMMING.

RIGHT: PATCHWORK IS THE ULTIMATE IN RECYCLED DRESSING.

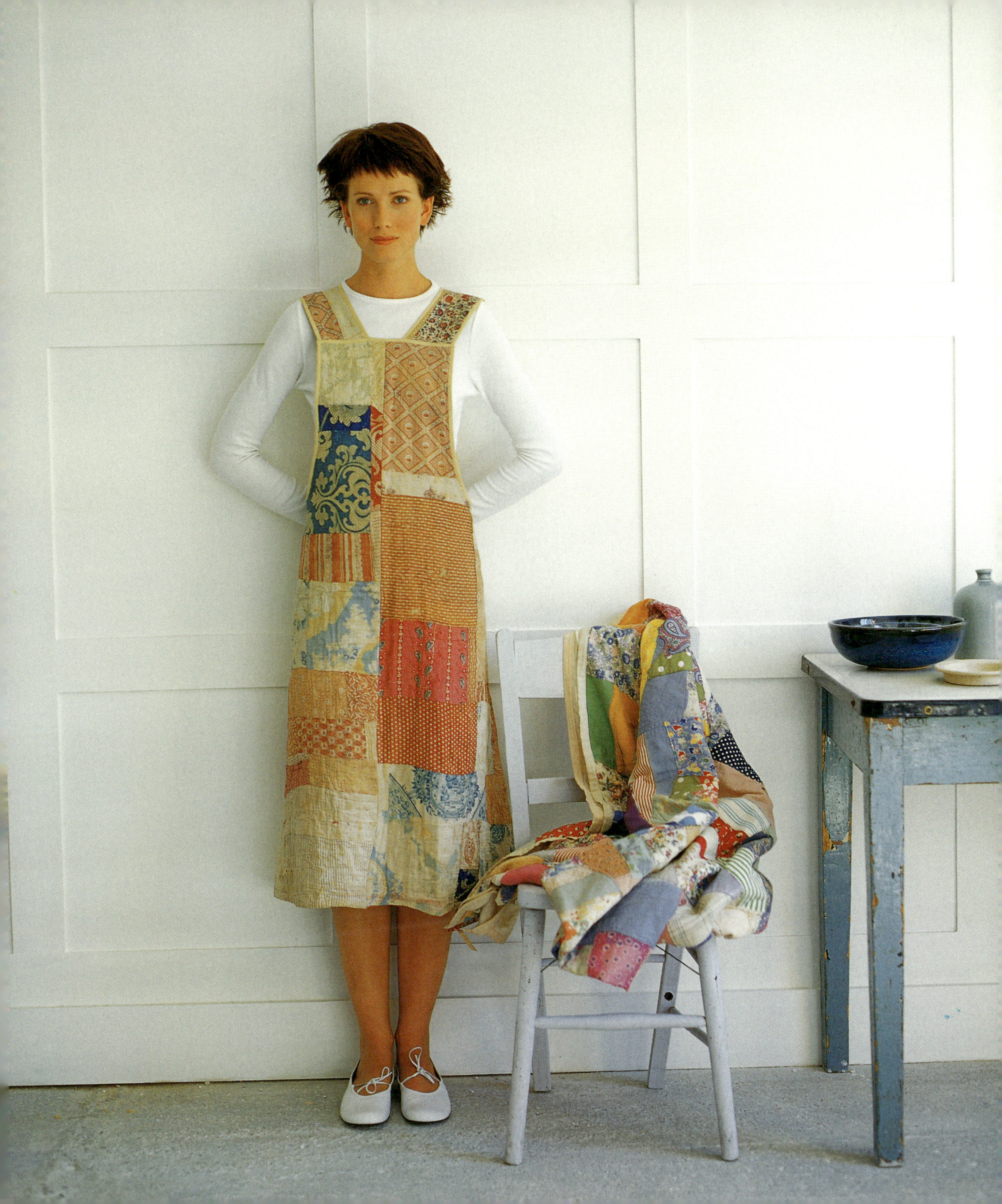

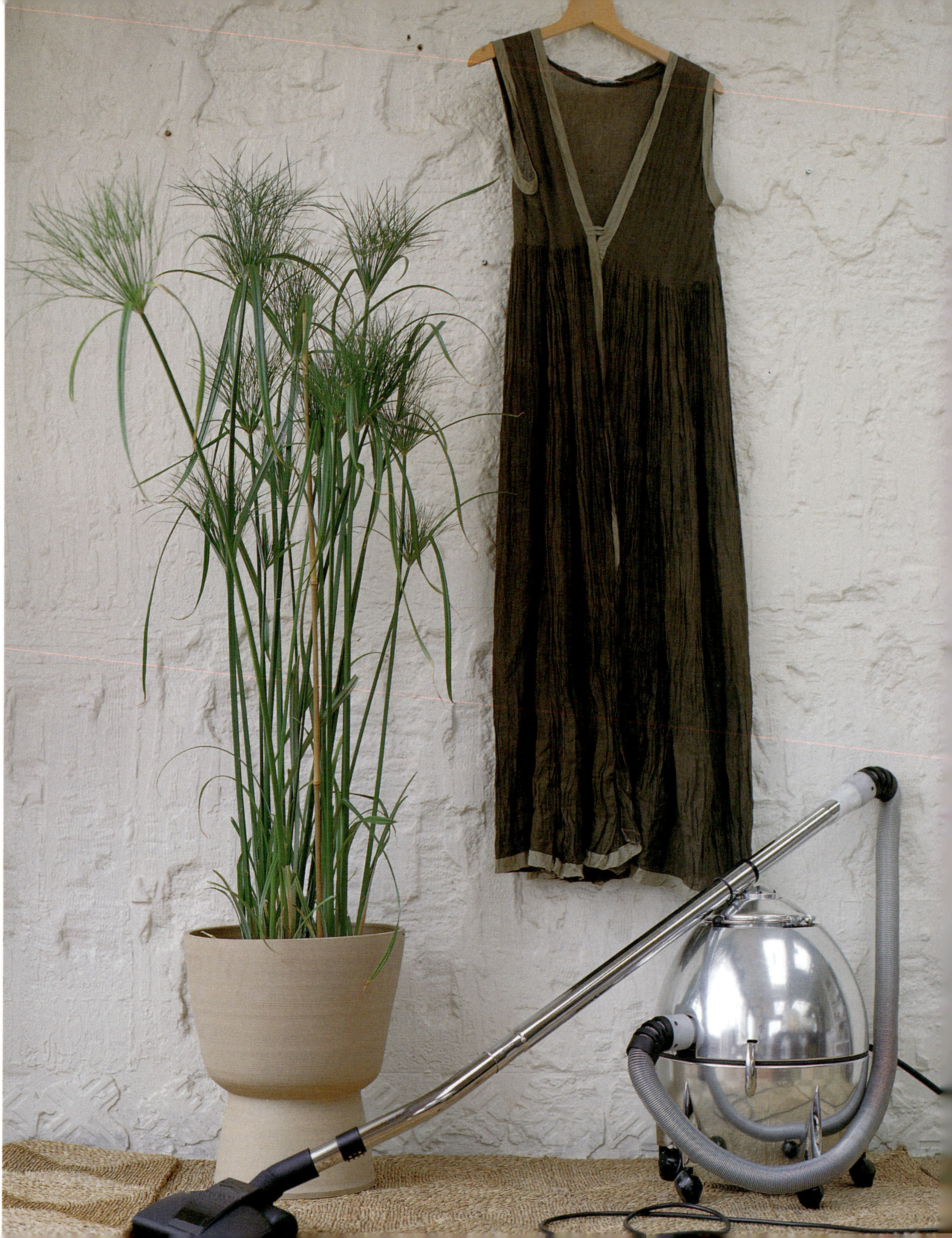

SYNTHETIC FABRICS

While most eco experts will tell you that all synthetic fabrics are bad, this is not strictly the case. Some materials, such as rayon, are manufactured from sustainable plant-based fibres and some of the newest arrivals on the scene are made from waste. Polartec, for example, uses recycled glass and is totally biodegradable, while fleece makes use of post-consumer plastic. As Susanna Glaser commented in *I.D.* magazine: 'A common misconception with technological advances in materials is that they somehow go against green issues and environmental concerns. But natural does not always mean planet-friendly ... [and] ... the fibres of synthetics can be pre-determined – leaving out environmentally unkind finishing treatments.' In California, for example, there is at least one company that is growing cotton with its own naturally produced colour, thus eliminating the dyeing process.

Some synthetic fabrics may even be good for your health. Micro-encapsulation, the technique of seeping millions of tiny chemical capsules into clothing, is the latest textile buzz word, allowing manufacturers to add beneficial ingredients to their products – be it vitamin C, sunscreen or natural remedies. From an environmental standpoint, the process is obviously controversial, but such nanotechnology has far-reaching implications for the future. As Glaser continues: 'By rearranging existing atoms, clothes and carpets could even be programmed to be self-replicating and self-cleaning.'

WHILE NYLON AND POLYESTER MAY MAKE THE ECO PURIST BLANCHE, SOME SYNTHETIC FIBRES ARE MORE ECO-FRIENDLY. WARM AND COLOURFUL FLEECE, FOR EXAMPLE, IS MADE OF RECYCLED PLASTIC AND SOME OF THE LATEST HI-TECH FABRICS EVEN CONTAIN ELEMENTS TO BENEFIT HUMAN HEALTH.

shoes

Made primarily from sustainable harvested hemp and natural latex – along with anything from recycled plastic bottles to polystyrene cups – 'organic' shoes are the ultimate in eco-friendly footwear. Look on the Internet for stylish suppliers and if you cannot find a look that you like, choose more conventional shoes or sandals in natural untreated leather or fabric. Modish shoe manufacturer Camper (recently awarded an ecological label) is worth keeping an eye on for good designs, such as hessian 'herbal' sandals – the natural solution for smelly feet.

ECO-FRIENDLY FOOTWEAR COMES IN MANY SHAPES AND SIZES. LOOK OUT FOR WOODEN CLOGS, HERBAL SANDALS AND SHOES MADE OF RECYCLED MATERIALS.

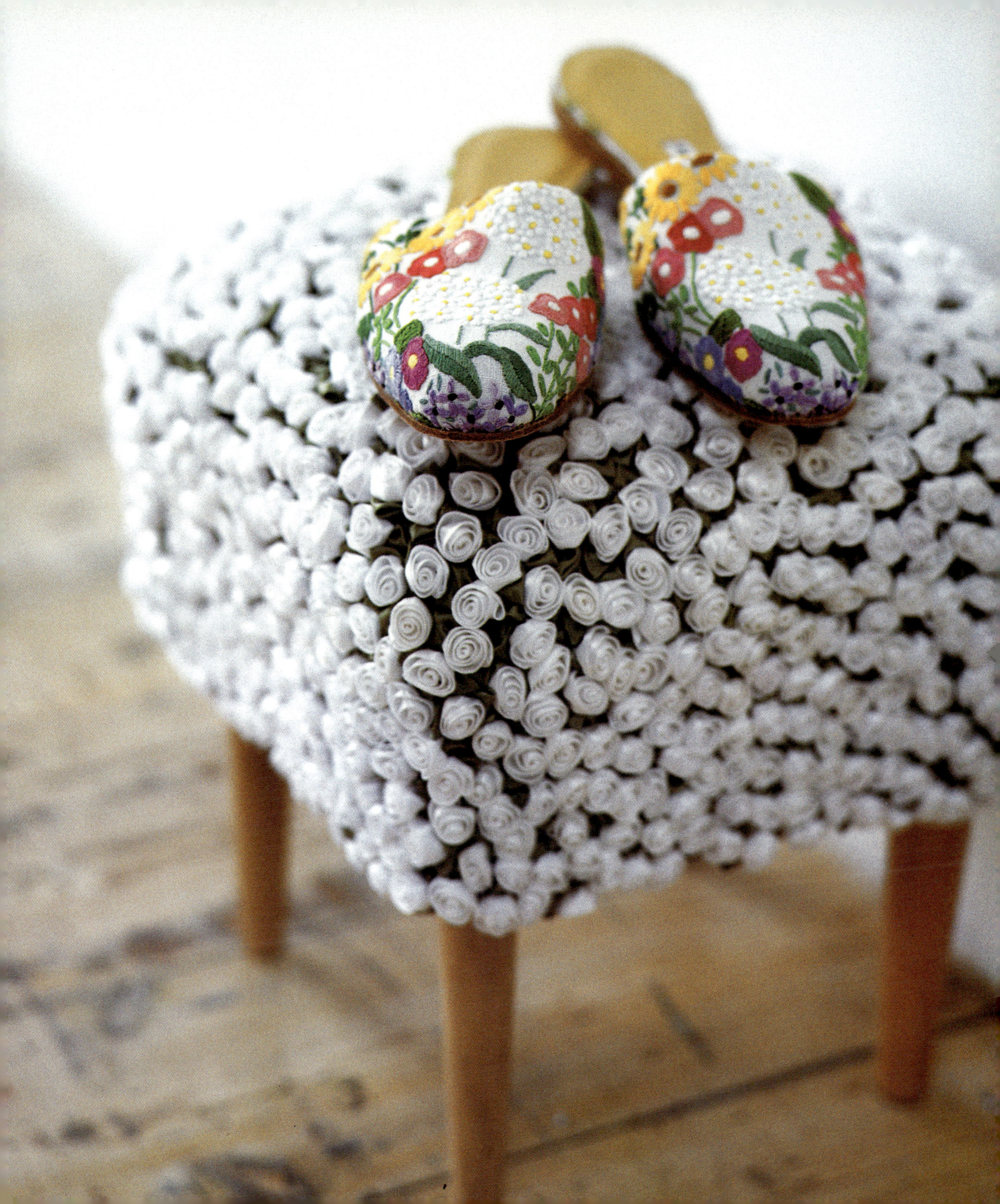

outdoors

Eco-living is not just about what happens inside the house; it's about the outside, too. It's about building a home which is in tune with the immediate environment, as well as the wider one; about using natural materials and organic shapes wherever possible; and it's about lessening the impact of our lives and our homes on the surroundings. So, whether you are building a house, an extension or a garden shed, think about its relationship with the natural world and make it a part of, rather than a blot on, the landscape. Our own outdoor space, too, comes into play here. As a mini part of the natural world, our gardens should work with it, rather than against it, and, however small, should be designed to be as organic and eco-friendly as possible.

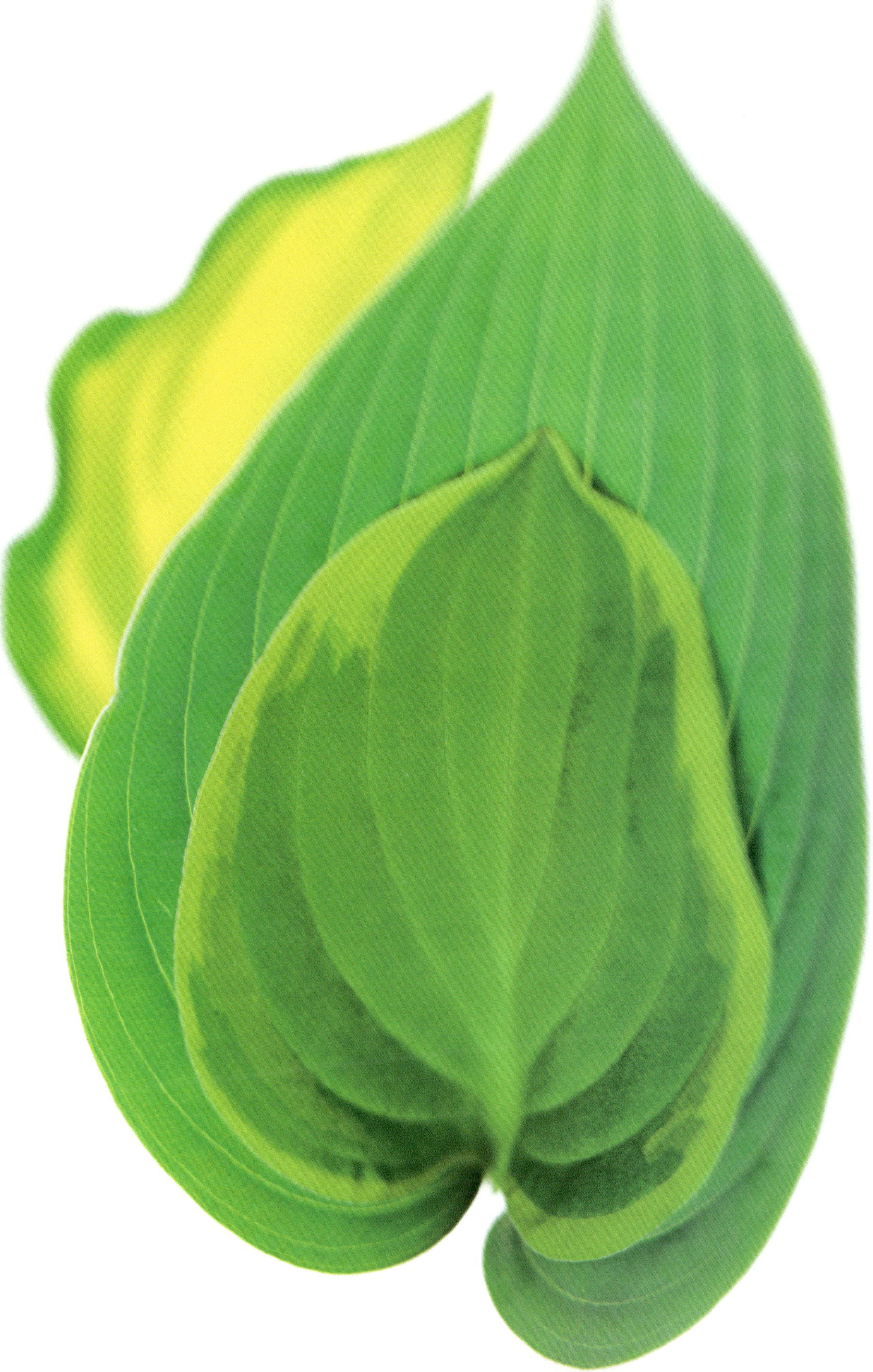

the house

The eco home is not just a style thing, it's an enduring way of life. So, if you are adapting your house or planning to construct a new one completely from scratch, it's important to consider the impact that every element of it will have on the environment.

These days, any architect with a conscience cannot fail to design with the environment in mind; a global movement towards 'green architecture' is gathering pace by the day. Some of its proponents do the bare minimum – simply creating buildings in organic shapes or placing more emphasis on using eco-friendly materials in construction. Others go much further – incorporating recycling systems for waste and rainwater in their designs, for example, or rejecting conventional non-renewable energy sources in favour of healthy and sustainable alternatives, such as solar power.

In terms of technology, the eco home is often streets ahead of its less worthy counterparts. And, more to the point, it can look just as chic and sophisticated – something that has done much to further its cause with the 'movers and shakers' of the contemporary design world who, it must be said, tend to be swayed by aesthetics rather than principles. While ten or fifteen years ago the idea of an environmentally friendly home would conjure up images of muddy hippie hangouts with compost toilets, the reality today is generally very different, with some of the best modern architecture combining green credentials with cutting-edge looks.

design

The eco home is not just a style thing, it's an enduring way of life. So, if you are adapting your house or planning to construct a new one completely from scratch, it's important to consider the impact that every element of it will have on the environment and attempt to make it blend in, rather than jar with the surrounding landscape. For starters, use building materials that are abundant and natural, choose energy systems that are harmless and sustainable, and think carefully about heat and water conservation. Building with an eco-conscience may take a bit of effort (eco builders merchants are fairly scarce for a start) and may cost you a little more at the outset, but the dividends to both you and the environment in the long run will be priceless.

MADE OF URBAN AND INDUSTRIAL SALVAGE (LEFT) OR SWEEPING ORGANIC FORMS (RIGHT), ECO BUILDINGS PROVIDE A PROTOTYPE FOR THE HOME OF THE FUTURE.

OUTDOORS 129

ECO BUILDING MATERIALS

Today's global economy and sophisticated transport systems mean that, in theory, we could build our homes out of anything – from tropical hardwood to Chinese marble. If we aim to be eco-friendly, however, we should not think along these lines. To save the energy and costs of transportation, to protect endangered natural resources and to make any new building look in keeping with its environment, it is preferable to build in vernacular style using local materials in the same way as our ancestors. Resources will obviously differ from location to location, but opt for natural materials such as timber, clay or stone, wherever you can.

Another eco option is to use salvaged or recycled materials for building. Ranging from the natural (old marine timber or stone from a deconsecrated church, for example) to the ex-industrial (corrugated iron, perhaps), these offer great aesthetic diversity – and can make for some highly individual results. Members of the Findhorn Foundation community in Scotland, for example, have turned old giant whisky barrels into comfortable contemporary homes.

As environmental issues become a matter of increasing public concern, eco builders merchants are springing up worldwide and new eco-friendly construction techniques are in the process of being developed. One such example is the Swiss-made Steko block system in which hollow wooden bricks are stacked up like Lego to make houses quickly, cheaply and with a reduced quantity of timber. But one of the most eco-friendly methods of construction is also one of the most ancient – building with straw bales – and it is taking off on both sides of the Atlantic. 'A straw house can have everything a modern house has but you hardly need central heating, the insulation is so good,' says one exponent.

WHY SUSTAINABLE TIMBER IS A MUST

To attain quantities of high-quality timber for buildings, paper and packaging, forests are being stripped alarmingly fast. According to Anna Kruger, in her book *H is for ecoHome*, 'Every second, one acre of irreplaceable tropical rainforest is being destroyed to satisfy the increasing demand for tropical hardwoods, to convert land to agriculture, and for cattle ranching. Commercial logging companies destroy or degrade an area of tropical forest equivalent in size to the UK annually.'

The environmental and climatic consequences of deforestation are only now being recognized. Cutting and burning forest releases huge amounts of carbon dioxide into the atmosphere, speeding up the greenhouse effect and global warming; it destabilizes the land, leading to soil erosion and flooding; and it destroys the habitat of indigenous peoples, as well as countless valuable plants and animals.

Sustainable forest management, which means regulated felling and replanting, is a solution, but only if it is done right. As David Pearson says in *The New Natural House Book*: 'The practice of replacing slow-growing deciduous forests (ie the hardwoods) with the faster-growing and therefore more profitable conifer plantations (ie the softwoods) places increasing demands on the import of hardwood, and causes the degradation of the landscapes from which they come.'

OUTDOORS 131

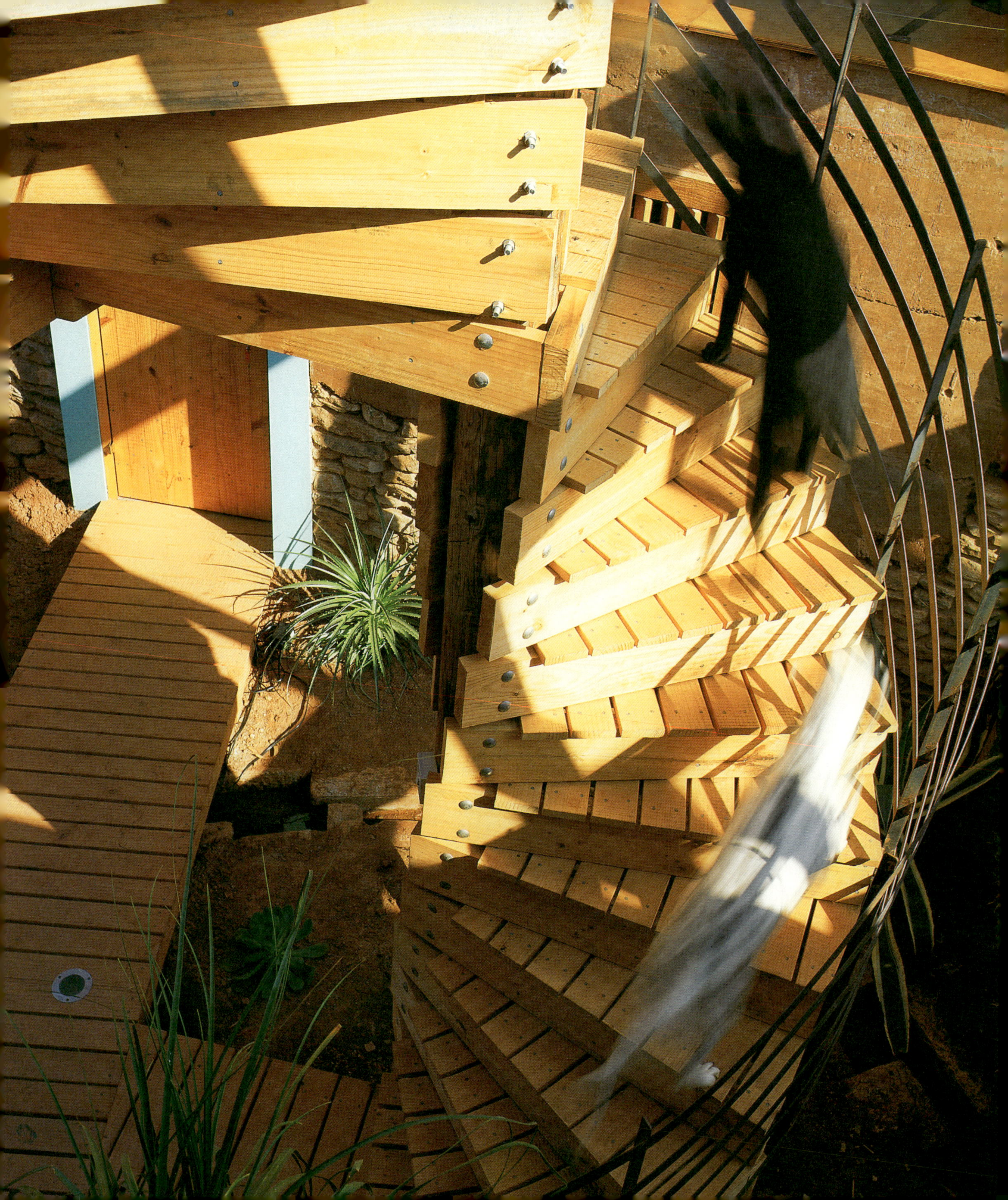

AN ECO HOME SHOULD IMPINGE
AS LITTLE AS POSSIBLE ON THE
SURROUNDING LANDSCAPE SO
THE MATERIALS USED SHOULD
BE LOCAL, NATURAL AND ECO-
FRIENDLY. THIS HOUSE IN LONDON
BY JOHN BROOME (SEE ALSO
PREVIOUS PAGES) IS SUPPORTED
SIMPLY WITH TREE TRUNKS – NOT
A FOUNDATION – AND THUS
CAUSES MINIMAL DISRUPTION
TO THE EARTH. SUSTAINABLE
TIMBER WORKS JUST AS WELL
INDOORS AS OUT (LEFT).

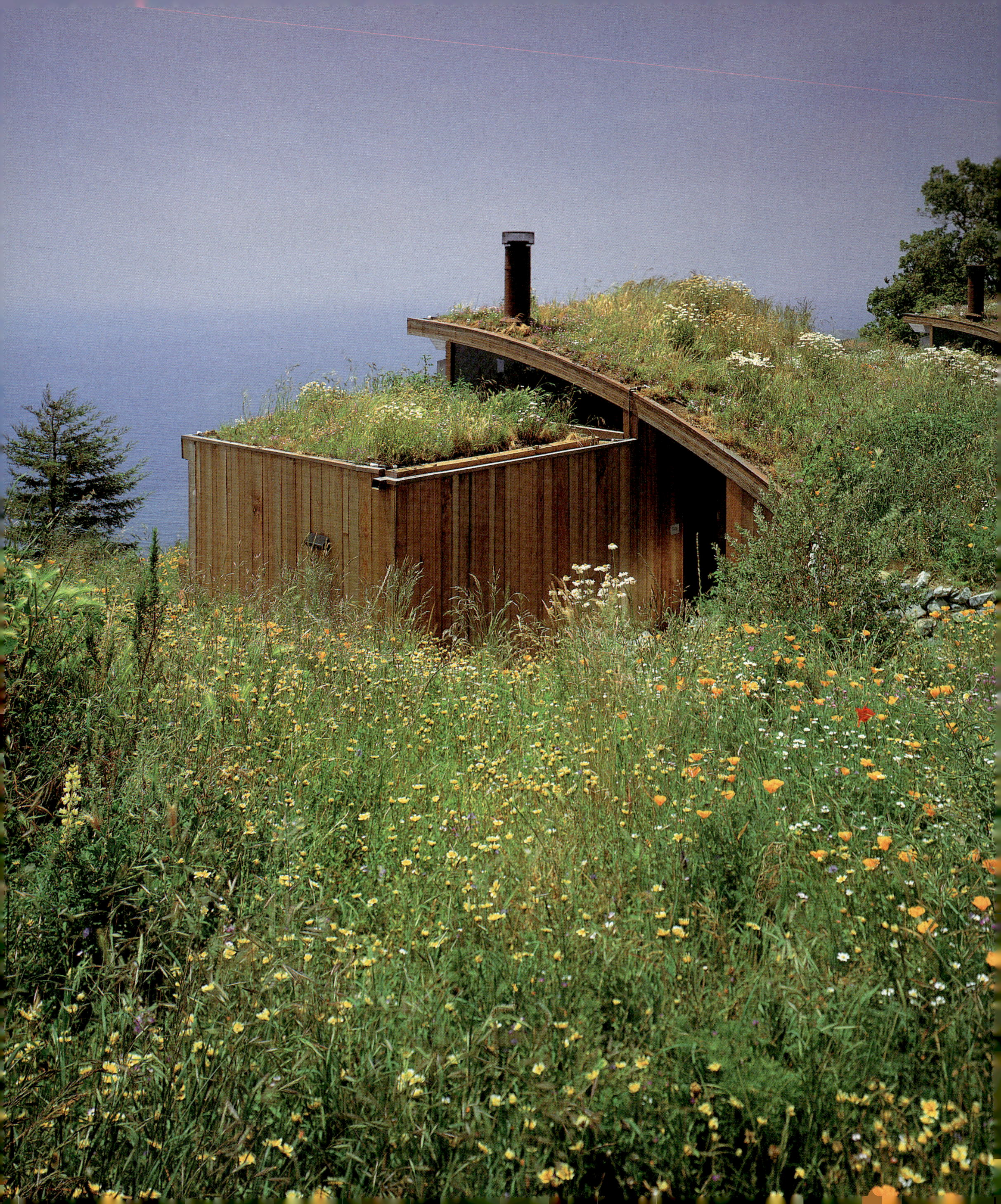

ENERGY IN THE HOME

At present, around three-quarters of the world's energy consumption comes from non-renewable sources – primarily oil, coal and natural gas. Our dependency on these 'hard-energy' sources is both shortsighted, since they will run out, and dangerous, since they all produce carbon dioxide, which damages the ozone layer and contributes to the greenhouse effect. Instead, we should be turning our attention to sustainable 'soft-energy' sources, such as sun, wind and water.

Harnessing the natural energy of wind and water is not generally thought to be a domestic option – it demands expensive equipment, for a start – but using the power of the sun for heating the home is a possibility. You can fit solar panels to the exterior of your house to heat both water and air, for example, or go for a more passive solar heating system. Solutions as simple as installing large high windows along a south-facing wall or creating a glass rooftop room (a more realistic alternative in the city) can work effectively, allowing greater amounts of sunlight to flood the interior. This passive way of harnessing the sun's energy can substantially reduce heating bills, particularly if the reflecting surfaces (walls and floors) are made of good insulating materials – concrete is excellent. High windows should keep the interior shaded during the summer, but if you have a glass sunspace, remember to make sure that you have adequate blinds, drapes or shutters to protect you during the hottest months.

The other key issue here is insulation. A vast amount of heat is lost through draughty windows, floors and doors, so by insulating your home properly – with natural materials, of course – you can conserve energy and save money. Best of all, top your home with a turf roof or even, if you are constructing a house from scratch, build part of it underground – as many of our ancestors did. Not only will it blend in with the environment, but the natural insulation of the earth will keep you cool in the summer and warm in the winter. Note, however, that any earth-sheltered home will need a very strong and waterproof roof.

PERFECT RETREATS FOR STRESSED-OUT URBANITES, THE GUEST BEDROOMS ARE EITHER DUG INTO THE WOODED HILLSIDE OR PERCHED ON STILTS IN TIMBER TREE HOUSES (BELOW) UNDER THE LEAVES.

THE POST RANCH INN AT BIG SUR, CALIFORNIA, DESIGNED BY ARCHITECT MICKEY MUENNIG, IS A TESTAMENT TO INNOVATIVE ECO ARCHITECTURE. THE MAIN RECEPTION (LEFT) IS HOUSED IN A BRILLIANTLY ENERGY-EFFICIENT MEADOW-TOPPED BUILDING WHICH HAS SPECTACULAR VIEWS ACROSS THE PACIFIC OCEAN.

WHERE DO WE GO FROM HERE?

Had we been asked 30 or so years ago what we thought the twenty-first century home would look like, most of us would have come up with space-age notions of silver capsules and hi-tech plastic pods. While organic shapes in building styles are becoming increasingly popular – look at British architect Nigel Coates's design for The Oyster House, for example (below right), or the very eco-chic pad belonging to BBC television's 'Teletubbies' – the most significant and forward-thinking modern architects are looking to nature rather than science for their inspiration.

In the search for a home that meets environmental concerns and yet satisfies our sophisticated domestic expectations, architects are responding with designs that attempt to marry the hi tech with the natural. Examples include curvy turf-topped dwellings that sit half underground, houses with top-to-bottom glass facades and adobe-style homes made of recycled rubbish and mud. Given the tremendous damage that is currently being caused to the environment by our consumer cultures in the Western world, it is vital that we develop from such ideas as these a prototype for a new kind of sustainable home – one that works with nature rather than against it. Clearly, eco building is the only way forward.

BELOW LEFT AND OPPOSITE: ARCHITECTURE IS LOOKING BACKWARDS TO GO FORWARDS, IT SEEMS. CAVE-LIKE AND ORGANIC, THESE BUILDINGS BY ARCHITECT JAVIER SENOSIAIN AGUILAR SEEM MORE AKIN TO TROGLODYTE DWELLINGS THAN THE HI-TECH SPACE-AGE CAPSULES WE MIGHT HAVE IMAGINED FOR THE FUTURE.

ABOVE: BRITISH ARCHITECT NIGEL COATES'S PROTOTYPE FOR THE HOUSE OF THE FUTURE – THE OYSTER HOUSE – IS BOTH CURVY AND ORGANIC.

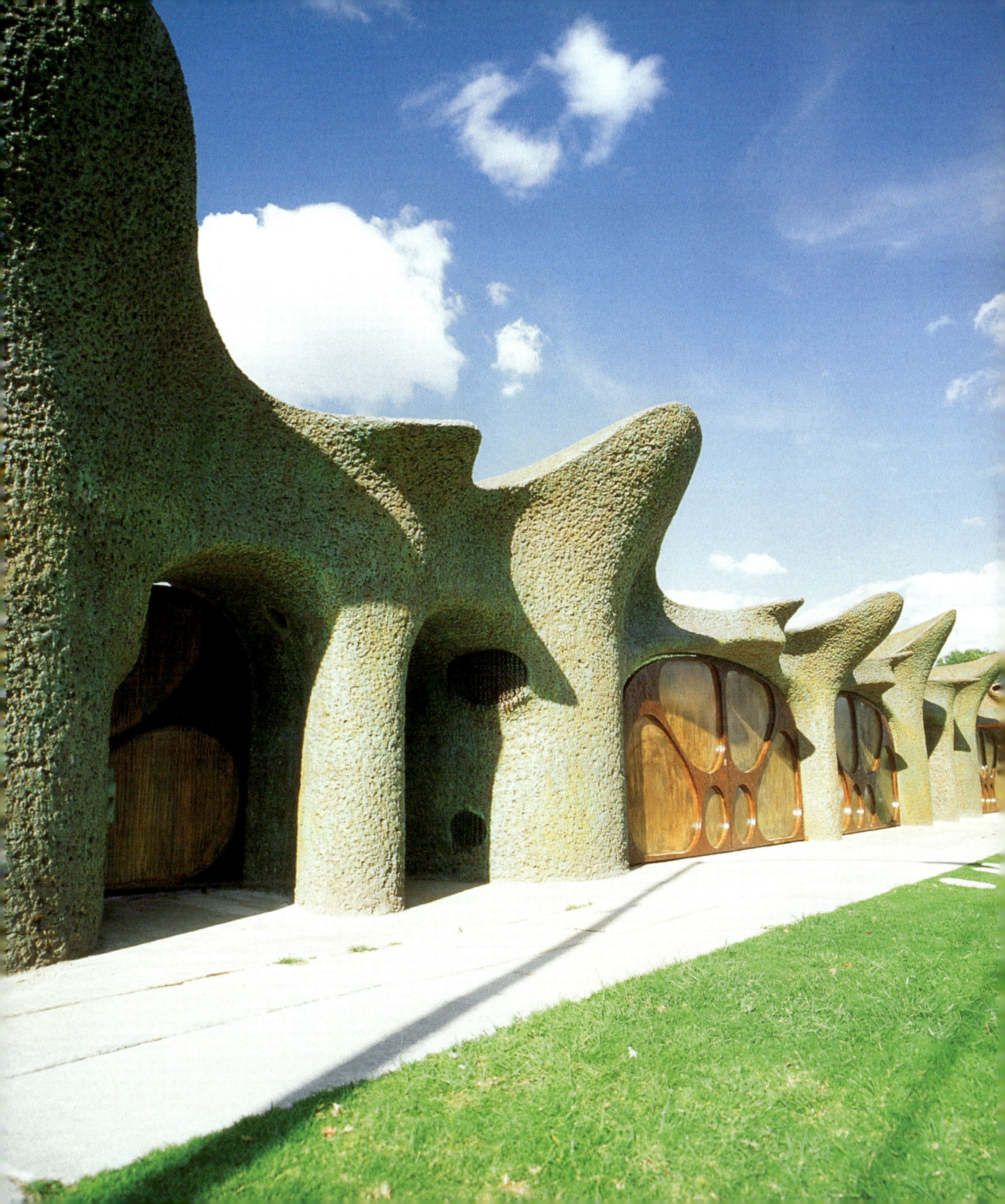

the garden

Eco-friendly gardening is not just about growing; there are countless other ways to be green outdoors. Whether you have a neat and tidy urban plot, a rambling country garden, or just a tiny roof terrace, try to incorporate some salvaged and recycled elements in its design. Be inspired by what is around you and choose materials that suit your surroundings.

Think organic and a garden is probably the first area of the home that springs to mind – a sweep of vegetable patch full of broad beans and broccoli, a wild orchard of apple and plum trees, a meadow of wild flowers. But eco-friendly gardening is not just about growing; there are countless other ways to be green outdoors.

design

Whether you have a neat and tidy cultivated urban plot, a large, rambling country garden, or just a tiny roof terrace with a few pots, try to incorporate some salvaged and recycled elements in the design of your outside space. Be inspired by what is around you and choose materials that suit your surroundings. In a seaside location, use lengths of driftwood for fencing, for example; in a city, turn old tin cans into funky flowerpots or use industrial corrugated iron for a cool garden shed. Ex-industrial containers also make good planters, so scour salvage yards for suitable ones. By adding such unexpected elements to your garden, you can make it eye-catching and individual as well as eco-friendly.

Don't forget the wider eco issues, either, when you come to design your garden. Keep tall trees away from the house so they don't block the sunlight from the interior; create a compost heap – if you have room – to make the most of your organic kitchen waste and invest in a water butt so you can recycle the rain and use it to water your plants and flowers.

FILM DIRECTOR DEREK JARMAN CREATED AN EXTRAORDINARY SCULPTURAL GARDEN NEXT TO HIS SEASIDE COTTAGE ON ENGLAND'S EAST COAST. REFLECTING THE BLEAK AND SURREAL LANDSCAPE THAT SURROUNDS IT, THE GARDEN IS A BRILLIANTLY MODERN MIX OF GRITTY SEASIDE SALVAGE AND BEAUTIFUL WILD FLOWERS.

GREEN GROWING

'Growing a garden, if you grow it organically, is improving a piece of the world,' says a recent catalogue from home furnishing store, Habitat UK. What's more, it will keep you in touch with the earth and in tune with nature. So, however small your plot, think of ways to produce good, wholesome and natural food on it. In a large garden, set aside an area for vegetable and fruit growing, and plant whatever appeals, be it broad beans and carrots, broccoli and beetroot, or radishes and rhubarb. With a little research and a fair bit of effort, you should be able to keep your larder filled with fresh organic produce throughout the year.

Don't go for the most common vegetable and fruit varieties. Pick the rarer ones if you can to ensure that they don't become extinct; in Europe this is a real concern as bureaucrats attempt to homogenize the seed production business. Neither should you be tempted to reach for the chemical sprays as soon as you spot a greenfly or other pest hovering around your vegetable patch. There are countless eco-friendly ways to fertilize and protect your crops, so read up on the subject and try to use alternatives where you can. Planting French marigolds among your vegetables, for example, is a good way of deterring white fly, while spraying plants with diluted washing-up liquid will do much to keep aphids away.

In a smaller garden, think carefully about how you can best maximize the growing potential. Squeeze rows of runner beans along a fence, for example, position a few pots of tomatoes in a sunny corner; a selection of herbs in a window box. Container gardening needn't limit your green fingers – cabbages, lettuces and even fruit trees can be successfully grown in pots and will give any urban backyard a taste of the wild.

IT IS EASY TO INCORPORATE ECO-FRIENDLY ELEMENTS INTO YOUR GARDEN. THIS PATH (ABOVE AND RIGHT) HAS BEEN FINISHED WITH RECYCLED BOTTLES, TURNED UPSIDE DOWN TO CREATE A GRAPHIC EDGING. ROUNDED POTS WILL BRING INSTANT ORGANIC LOOKS TO A TERRACE (LEFT), BUT TO BE REALLY ECO, GROW YOUR OWN ORGANIC PRODUCE (RIGHT).

home-grown

Resources

BEAUTY, CLEANSING & NATURAL HEALTH

Dr Hauschka: (01527) 832863 (UK); 800-247 9907 (US); 029-660-2555 (Australia).

Farmacia, 169 Drury Lane, London WC2B 5QA, (020) 7831 0830 and branches.

Fresh & Wild, 210 Westbourne Grove, London W11 2RH, (020) 7229 0468.

Green People: (01444 401444).

Jurlique: (020) 8841 6644.

Napiers Dispensary, 18 Bristol Place, Edinburgh EH1 1EZ, (0131) 225 5542.

The Nutri Centre, 7 Park Crescent, London W1N 3HE, (020) 7436 5122.

Planet Organic, 42 Westbourne Grove, London W2 5SH, (020) 7221 7171.

Wild Oats Wholefoods, 210 Westbourne Grove, London W11 2RH, (020) 7229 0468.

BOOKS

Counsell, Simon, *The Good Wood Guide*, London, Friends of the Earth, 1996. (Available in Australia from Wilderness Society and in the USA as *The Smart Wood Guide*, Rainforest Alliance.)

Foley, Tricia, *The Natural Home*, London, Pavilion Books, 1995.

Hall, Keith & Warm, Peter, *Greener Building*, Llandysull, AECB, 1998. (To order, call (01559) 370908.)

Kruger, Anna, *H is for EcoHome*, London, Gaia Books, 1991. (Also *G is for EcoGarden* and *R is for Reuse, Repair, Recycle*.)

Markham, Gavin, *The Green Guide*, London, Gavin Markham (nine regional editions, published annually). (For a copy, call (020) 7354 2709.)

Papanek, Victor, *The Green Imperative*, London, Thames & Hudson, 1995.

Pearson, David, *The New Natural House Book*, London, Conran Octopus, 1998.

Talbot, John, *Simply Build Green*, Findhorn, Findhorn Press, 1997. Call (01309) 690110 for further information, or contact The Foundation Community on (01309) 672 288 or at www.findhorn.org

Woolley, Tim, Kimmins, Sam & Harrison, Paul, *The Green Building Handbook*, London, Spon, 1997 (Available from Construction Resources, see below.)

BUILDING MATERIALS

Construction Resources, 16 Great Guildford Street, London SE1 0HS, 020 7450 2211, email: info@ecoconstruct.com.

Ecological Building Society, The (0345) 697758. (For eco mortgages.)

EcoTech, 10111 Nelson Street, Westminster, Colorado 80021, USA, 00 1 303/465-1537.

Environmental Construction Products, 26 Millmoor Road, Meltham, Huddersfield, W. Yorks. HD7 3JY, (01484) 854 898.

Kunz GmbH & Co, postfach 61, D-74415 Gschwend, Federal Republic of Germany, + 49.7972.690 and Kucospan Sales UK, Peveral House, The Green, Hatfield Peveral, Essex CM3 2JF, (01245) 382 168. (For eco-friendly chipboard.)

CLOTHING, FABRICS & SHOES

Camper: (020) 7584 5439.

Greenfibres, Freepost LON 7805, Totnes, Devon, 01803 868001. (Call for a mail-order catalogue.)

Hess Naturtextilien GmbH, 00 49 6033 991 142 (For hemp wedding dresses.)

DESIGN & DECORATION

Auro Organic Paints Supplies Ltd, Unit 1, Goldstones Arm, Ashdon, Essex CB10 2LZ, (01799) 584888.

Eco Interiors, 40 Heathfield North, Twickenham, Middlesex TW2 7QW, (020) 8892 2397.

Livos Natural Paints & Timber Care, The Nature Maid Company, Unit D7, Maws Craft Centre, Jackfield, Ironbridge, Shrops. TF8 7LS, (01952) 883288.

Nutshell Natural Paints, Hamlyn House, Buckfastleigh, TQ11 0NR, (01364) 642892 and nuts@nutshellpaints.freeserve.co.uk.

World of Difference, 14 Woburn Walk, London WC1H 0JL, (020) 7387 2363.

FLOORING

Forbo-Nairn, PO Box 1, Kirkcaldy, KY1 2SB, Scotland, (01592) 643777 and www.forbo-nairn.co.uk (For lino.)

Noraplan, Norament, Ecoplan and Ecoment flooring by German company Freudenberg. Call (01455) 261240. (For rubber.)

Wicanders Amorim (UK), Star Road, Partridge Green, Horsham, West Sussex, RH13 8RA, (01403) 710001. (For cork.)

FOOD & DRINK

Fresh & Wild, see above.

Planet Organic, see above

Wild Oats Wholefoods, see above.

LIGHTING

Archimoon Eco light by Philippe Starck, produced by Flos. For UK stockists, call 020 7258 0600; for US stockists, call (516) 549-2745.

Artemide GB Limited, 106 Great Russell Street, London WC1B 3RJ (Call (020) 7631 5200 for further information about the E-light featured on page 81).

ORGANIZATIONS

Centre for Alternative Technology, Machynlleth, Powys. SY20 9AZ, (01654) 702400.

Ecological Design Association, (01453) 765575

Friends of the Earth, 26–28 Underwood Street, London N1 7JG, (020) 7490 1555.

Soil Association, Bristol House, 40–56 Victoria Street, Bristol BS1 6BY, (0117) 929 0661.

SHOPPING

Felissimo, 10 West 56th Street, NYC, 00 1 212-956 4438.

Natural Collection, Eco House, 19a Monmouth Place, Bath BA1 2DQ, (01225) 442288. (Mail order natural and organic products for the home.)

Out Of This World, call (0191) 213 5377 for branches in Cheltenham, Newcastle and Nottingham. (Organic food, bodycare, stationery etc.)

Terra Verde Trading Corporation, 120 Wooster Street, New York, NY 10012-5200, 001 212-925-4533.

WEBSITES

www.aecb.net (Association for Environmentally Conscious Building)

www.camper.es. (For shoes.)

www.ecodecor.co.uk (Training in eco-friendly design.)

www.foe.co.uk (Friends of the Earth)

www.holidaybank.co.uk/tourops/eco.htm: (Holidays and tours with an ecological emphasis.)

www.living-foods.com): (The living and raw foods website.)

www.soilassociation.org

www.wildoats.com: (Particularly useful for wild links.)

Index

Figures in italics indicate captions.

accessories
    bathroom 85, 90, *90*
    kitchen 16, *17*
    living room 58, *61*
    office *70*
acupuncture 107, *107*
aluminium 16
armchairs 46, 49, 61
aromatherapy 102, *102*
art 62
Art Nouveau 36
audio-equipment 65
Ayurveda 107

bamboo 36, 44, 111
basins *86*, 90
baskets 58
bathing 82–107
    bathroom design 85
    complementary medicine 100–107
    eco beauty 96–9
    eco cleansing 92–5
    hardware 86–9
    software 90, *90*
baths 82, 87, *89*, 90
beauty products 96–9
bedrooms 108–17
    beds 111, *112*
    blankets 116
    design 111
    duvets and pillows 112
    mattresses 112
    quilts 116, *117*
    sheets 111, *114*, 115
blankets 116
bowls *11*, 16, 52
breeze blocks 52, *52*

carpets 44, 69
ceramics 12, *54*, 85
chairs 39, *46*, 49, 52, 70
cleaning 19
clothing 108, 118–25
    fabrics 119–20
    fur, skin and leather 120
    shoes 124, *124*
    synthetic fabrics 123, *123*
complementary medicine 100–107
computers 69, 73, *73*, 74
concrete 85, *89*
cookers 11, 18
cookware 16
cork 40, 44, 85, 111
crystals 107
curtains 57, 58, *113*
cushions 57, 90
cutlery *17*

daybeds 61
deodorants 95
desks 70
diet 27, 98
dishwashers 18–19
drink 30–35
duvets 112

electromagnetic fields (EMF) 49, 65

fabrics 40, *54*, 57, *57*, 119–20
    synthetic 123, *123*
felt 40, *45*, 111
feng shui 49, 111
floors 12, 44, *45*, 85
food 20–29
    the cost question 26
    functional 106
    the health issue 27
    organic 21, 26, 27
    packaging 26
    what to eat 21
    where to shop 25
    year-round choice 26
    see also recipes
Forest Stewardship Council (FSC) 44
freezers 19
fridges 19
Friends of the Earth 44, 65
furnishings 56–63
furniture
    bio 46, 49
    driftwood 36
    eco-friendly 49
    office 66, 69, 70, *70*
    plastic 49
    rattan 36, 49
    recycled materials 51–2
futons 111

garden, the 126, 139–41
    design 139, *139*
    green growing 140, *140*
glass 16, *35*, 49, 85, 136
granite 12
green movement 7
green tea *35*
greenhouse effect 19
Greenpeace 119

hardwoods 12, 44, 130, 131
heating 65, *65*

herbalism 105, *105*
homeopathy 101
house, the 126, 128–37
    design 129
    eco building materials 130–33
    energy in the home 135, *135*
    the future 136, *136*
insulation 85, 130, 135
International Federation of Organic Agricultural Movements (IFOAM) 21
ionizers 65, 74
iridology 107

Japanese cuisine 27
juices 31

kitchens 10–19
    accessories and cookware 16
    aluminium 16
    eco cleaning 19
    floors and surfaces 11–15
    green machines 18–19
    thinking green 16

laminates 44
lamps *48*, 51
lighting 81, *81*
linoleum 44
living rooms 36–65
    design 39
    floors 44, *45*
    furniture and furnishings 46–63
    recycling 51–2
    walls 39–41
loose covers 57

massage 107
matting 36, 39, 44, *45*, 52
mattresses 111, 112
metals 49
micro-encapsulation 123
milk 35
mosaic 12, *86*

packaging 11, 16, 26, 58, 62, 92
paints 40, *41*, 69
particleboards 15
pillows 112
plants 52, 58, 69, *69*, 74, 111
plastics 15, *15*, 16, *17*, 39, 49, 51, 85, 90
plates 16, *17*
plywoods 15, 44

quilts 116, *117*

recipes
    apple kick 32

enticer 33
Nigella Lawson's pavlova 28
power boost 32
Renée Elliott's favourite salad 27
sparkling memory 33
Reiki 107
resources 142
rubber 44
rubbish 19, 62, 66, *74*, 136
rugs 111, 116

screens *15*
scrubs 92, *95*
sculptures 62, *62*
shampoos 98
sheets 111, *114*, 115
shoes 124, *124*
shopping 25
showers 85, 87
skincare 95
smoothies 31
soaps 92, *92*, 95, *95*
softwoods 131
Soil Association, The 21
Space Age 36
steel 12, 84
stone 12, *12*, 85, *86*

tables 49, 52
tableware *17*
taps 89
tiles 12, 40, *86*
toilets 89, 90
toothpaste 95

varnishes 41, 44
vases 58, *61*
vinyl 44

wallpaper 36, 39
washing machines 11, 18
washing powders 18, *19*
water 35
wheatgrass 35, 58
windows 58, 69
wood 12, 40–41, 44, *54*, 85, *89*, 90, 111, 130, 131, *133*
working 66–81
    design 69
    equipment 72–5
    ergonomics 69, *69*, 70
    lighting 81, *81*
    office supplies 76–9
worktops *11*, 12, 15

Picture credits

The publishers would like to thank the following sources for their kind permission to reproduce the pictures in this book:

Artemide E Light 020 7631 5200 for enquiries, 81
Jane Atfield *Made of Waste*, 15
Graham Atkins-Hughes, 38
Graham Atkins-Hughes/© Carlton Books Ltd, 5, 99, 102, 103
Graham Atkins-Hughes/*Living etc*/IPC Syndication, 75
Benetton paint colours and effect finishes, B&Q 0800 444840, 40, 41, 46, 112bl
Dominic Blackmore/*Family Circle*/IPC Syndication, 70tr
Dominic Blackmore/*Homes & Ideas*/IPC Syndication, 79
Mirjam Bleeker/Taverne Agency. Production: Frank Visser, 2/3, 12tr, 12br, 13
Jennifer Cawley, 86tl
Nigel Coates, Concept sketch of Oyster house, by Nigel Coates 1998., 136r
The Conran Shop/Conran Collection 020 7589 7401, 25l
Chris Craymer. Location: Jibby Beane's shell-like apartment in Clerkenwell, designed by Jibby in 1997, 17, 50, 60, 63, 124
Chris Craymer, 47
Matthew Donaldson, 20, 26tl, 26bl, 48, 49b, 51, 52tl, 52tr, 53, 55, 112tl, 122
C Drake/*Living etc*/IPC Syndication, 70br
Cath Kidston/*Vintage Style*/Ebury Press/Pia Tryde, 76, 116
Craig Fraser, 18–19, 58tl, 59, 64, 70
Rene Gonkel. Styling: Marjolein Padhos, 69, 84, 85, 86bl, 89
Zoe Hope Textiles, 57, 118
Janine Hosegood/© Carlton Books Ltd, 19, 35, 65, 74, 77, 78tl, 78bl, 80, 91, 92tl, 92br, 95, 97tl, 97tr, 98tl, 119, 120l, 120r, 123l
Sandro Hyams, 96
The Image Bank, 105br, 105tr
International Archives/Paul Ryan, 45br
Christoph Kicherer. Architect: Javier Senosian, 42, 43, 87, 129
Tom Leighton/Elizabeth Whiting Associates, 61t, 61b, 125
Alex Macdonald. Styling: Claire Hunt, 101
Mainstream Photography/Ray Main, 14, 16tr, 45cr, 52bl, 72, 90tl, 90bl, 113, 115
Mainstream/Designer: Isokon, 16bl
Mainstream/Designer: Roger Oates, 45tl
Mainstream/Architect: John Broome, 130, 131, 133
Mainstream/Architect: David Sheppard, 132
Mainstream/Garden: Phil Rookesby, 140tl, 140br
J P Masclet/*Living etc*/ IPC Syndication, 121
Andrew Moran 25bl, 25br, 25tr, 27
Muji – 020 832 32208, Copyright Ryohin Keikaku Co. Ltd. Trading as Muji, 78
Roger Oates Design – 020 735 12288, 45bl, 45tr
Fleur Olby, 1, 9, 29 (courtesy of Nigella Lawson), 30, 31, 32, 34, 37, 67, 73, 83, 94, 100, 104, 109, 127
The Organic Picture Library/Geoff Wilkinson, 4, 22, 24, 141
Peter Saunders © *Brides* and *Setting up Home*/The Condé Nast Publications, 93
Anne Selim handwoven textiles, 56
Javier Senosiain 136bl, 137
Anne Soderberg. Styling: Pepe Leal. Location: Ray Harris, 3, 68
Howard Sooley, 138, 139
Space Boudoir – 214 Westbourne Grove, London W11 2RH. 020 722 96533, 114, 117t, 117b
Tim Street Porter, 134, 135
William Taylor, 123r
Chris Tubbs/*Living etc*/IPC Syndication, 111
Alexander Van Berge/Taverne Agency. Styling: Stef Bakker, 45cl, 54tl, 54br, 140bl
Verne/Architect: Obumex – John Pawson, 10, 11
Verne/Architect: Glen Sestig, 71
Verne/Architect: Vincent Van Duyson, 86, 110
Verne/Architect: Nathalie Van Reeth, 88
Paul Warchol Photography, 39, 128
Luke White, 23, 49tr
Polly Wreford/© Carlton Books Ltd, 106
Xavier Young, 6
Paul Zak © *Vogue*/The Condé Nast Publications, 107
Elizabeth Zeschin. Sculpture by Carol Sinclair, 62

Every effort has been made to acknowledge correctly and contact the source and/or copyright holder of each picture, and Carlton Books Limited apologizes for any unintentional errors or omissions which will be corrected in future editions of this book.

Front Cover: Janine Hosegood

Back Cover: Courtesy of Eco Composting Ltd. Enquiries 01202 593601. Eco Composting operate the largest purpose-built green waste composting facility in the UK and produce a range of sustainable composts, mulches and enriched soils.

Acknowledgements

The author and publisher have made every effort to ensure that all information on the use of herbal products and essential oils is correct and up-to-date at the time of publication. However, the application and quality of herbal products and essential oils is beyond the control of the above parties, who cannot be held responsible for any problems resulting from their use.

Do not use herbal products or essential oils without prior consultation with a qualified aromatherapist if you are pregnant, taking any form of medication, or if you suffer from oversensitive skin. Half-doses of essential oils should always be used for children and the elderly.

Neither the author nor the publisher can accept responsibility for any accident, injury or damage that results from using the ideas, information or advice offered.

SOURCES & REFERENCES

Chapter 1 For kitchen design and green machines: *H is for ecoHome* by Anna Kruger, published by Gaia Books Ltd, 1991, and *The New Natural House Book* by David Pearson, published by Conran Octopus, 1998.

For food: *Homes & Gardens* February 2000, p 104. The Soil Assocation website at www.soilassociation.org. Recipe on p 28 copyright © Nigella Lawson 1999, first published in the *Observer* magazine, June 27, 1999.

For juice and wheatgrass information: the living and raw foods website (www.livingfoods.com). (Three recipes on pp 32–3.)

For milk: nutritionist Patrick Holford of the Institute for Optimum Nutrition in Putney, London quoted in Hazel Courteney's What's the Alternative? column, in the *Style* section of *The Sunday Times*, January 18 1998.

Chapter 2 For wallcoverings: *H is for ecoHome* by Anna Kruger, published by Gaia Books Ltd, 1991.

For wood veneers: *Building for a Future* magazine, Summer/Autumn 1998, p 14.

For paints: fact sheet 41 from Construction Resources, see Resources, and *The New Natural House Book* by David Pearson, published by Conran Octopus, 1998.

For furniture: Recycling catalogue which accompanied a British craft touring exhibition of the same name.

For furnishings: *H is for ecoHome*, by Anna Kruger, published by Gaia Books, 1991 and *The New Natural House Book* by David Pearson, published by Conran Octopus, 1998. Also, 'Manic Organic', an article on Javier Senosiain Aguiler's Mexican house published in *Elle Decoration* 53 (October 1996), p 80.

Chapter 3 For eco techno: *The New Natural House Book* by David Pearson, published by Conran Octopus, 1998. The website of Debra Lynn: www.dld123.com.

For eco office kit and lighting: *The New Natural House Book* by David Pearson, published by Conran Octopus, 1998.

Chapter 4 For the hardware: *H is for ecoHome* by Anna Kruger, published by Gaia Books Ltd, 1991, and *The New Natural House Book* by David Pearson, published by Conran Octopus, 1998.

For eco cleansing: the catalogue for Green People, see Resources. *H is for ecoHome* by Anna Kruger, published by Gaia Books Ltd, 1991. The website for soapnuts at www.soapnut.com.

For eco beauty: catalogue for Green People, see Resources. 'Back to Nature', an article by Jane Preston in *Marie Claire* (UK), April 2000. www.frugalliving.about.com (home-made skincare treatments taken from here).

For Hair: *Herbs for Health and Healing* Copyright © 1996 by Rodale Inc. from website: www.naturesapothecary.com (*Mother Nature Encyclopaedia of Natural Health*).

For complementary medicine: 'Healing in Harmony', an article by Jerome Burne, published in the *Guardian* weekend supplement, February 26, 2000. *Essential Energy* by Nikki Goldstein, published by Warner Books, 1997. *The Body Shop Book of Wellbeing*, published by Ebury Press, 1998. *Aveda Rituals* by Horst Rechelbacher, published by Owl Books, 1999. Hazel Courteney's What's the Alternative? column in the *Style* section of *The Sunday Times*.

Chapter 5 For beds and sheets: *H is for ecoHome* by Anna Kruger, published by Gaia Books Ltd, 1991. *The New Natural House Book* by David Pearson, published by Conran Octopus, 1998.

For synthetic fabrics: 'Tech-style', an article by Susanna Glaser which appeared in *i-D* magazine.

Chapter 6 For eco-building materials: fact sheet from Construction Resources (Steko blocks) – see Resources. 'Eco Houses', an article by Elspeth Thompson in *Elle Decoration* 56 (February 1997). 'Whisky Galore', an article by Tamsin Blanchard in the *Observer* magazine, June 27, 1999.

For energy in the home: *The New Natural House Book* by David Pearson, published by Conran Octopus. 'On an Eco Trip to California', article by Jack Flowers in *Elle Decoration* 63 (October 1997).

The author also wishes to thank:

Nigel Russell at Construction Resources and Renée Elliott at Planet Organic for their help.

Jo Lethaby and Alice Whately for editing the text so efficiently.

Abi Dillon for inspired and exhaustive picture research.

Zia Mattocks, Venetia Penfold and Penny Stock at Carlton Books for making it happen.

Clive, Ella, India and Müge for everything.